FLU PANDEMIC 1918

THE GREAT INFLUENZA OF THE LAST CENTURY. HISTORY, CONSEQUENCES AND TREATMENT IN THE WORLD OF THE 1920'S

By

STEPHEN RYAN

Table of Contents

Introduction

U nderstanding the world in which the influenza pandemic took hold is pivotal to understanding why it spread as it did as well as why individuals and societies responded in the way they did. The biggest and most prestigious global event in 1918 was World War I, which began four years earlier and had already killed millions of soldiers and civilians.

By 1918, the war was still fierce on both sides, and while the Allied forces (mainly Great Britain, France, and the United States) had begun to turn the tide of the war, a clear victor had not yet definitively emerged. The entry of the United States into the war helped bring about the Allied victory, but in January 1918, their impact was not, however, felt. What was more, at the time of the declaration of war, the United States had under 150,000 men enlisted, so a massive mobilization needed to take place? Finally, although the war was declared against Germany in April, they did not pass a declaration of war against Austria-Hungary, Germany's ally, until December 1917.

Soldiers from Germany traveled to France; Japanese sailors sailed to the Mediterranean Sea; Austrian forces invaded Serbia; Arabians fought alongside the British; and so on, until so many people came in contact with others, they never would have otherwise met. Then, they went home. This massive movement of people made it possible for the disease to foster among them. The fact that the war wound down throughout 1918, and a truce was reached in November, also meant that throughout the year, many of these men and women went home. With them went the influenza germs to nearly every corner of the globe. This allowed the pandemic to spread much more rapidly than it otherwise would have in the early twentieth century.

The war was a factor in other ways as well. Disease outbreaks in combat are also to be expected; in nearly every battle in global history, thousands (if not millions) of combatants die of disease, be it gangrene, typhoid, influenza, or a myriad of other illnesses. Thus, wartime doctors and hospitals did not immediately recognize the 1918 influenza strain as especially virulent or a significant threat to civilians.

Besides, the war caused many other disruptions that made the world, especially Europe, vulnerable to the disease. The war had ravaged the city and countryside alike. Many places lay in ruins by 1918, and rebuilding had yet to begin since the war was still ongoing. This meant that many civilians were homeless or displaced, having been forced to flee, which inevitably impacted their overall health and ability to fight a virus. Many were grouped in makeshift dwellings, bringing them in closer contact with others, sometimes without ideal sanitation.

Troops had marched through many areas as well, either confiscating or destroying livestock and food. The typical workforce needed to maintain food supplies were also diminished because so many fought (and died or were injured) in the war. Food supply chains were disrupted or destroyed by the war. Starvation in parts of Europe was widespread during World War I, perhaps killing millions. And again, for those who did not perish, malnutrition diminished their ability to fight influenza once they were exposed to it.

In addition to the war, the Russian Revolution was ongoing, affecting millions of people in Eastern Europe. The revolution began in early 1917, so it was well underway and had caused great upheaval by the time the virus struck in 1918. Russia suffered massive casualties in the first few years of World War I, to the extent that many in the military were ready to mutiny. Also, starvation was widespread across the Russian Empire, increasing already left-leaning tendencies among the large urban working class and rural farm laborers, many of whom were still stuck in virtual serfdom.

In the months of 1917, after the Russian tsar abdicated and Parliament assumed control, on the local level, the urban working poor and soldiers began to unite and form "Soviets" in rebellion against Parliament. Also, several territories of the Russian Empire rose in revolt, including Belarus, Armenia, Lithuania, Estonia, Azerbaijan, and Ukraine. Great upheaval and disruption occurred, making populations more vulnerable to the influenza outbreak to come.

Even in places not directly impacted by fighting and unrest, conditions existed that nurtured the virus. Poverty and overcrowding in cities worldwide were rampant. The global industry prioritized production for war. Many healthcare workers were deployed overseas to care for the massive war casualties. Also, knowledge about disease transmission, prevention, and hygiene was not widespread.

As is apparent, when 1918 began, and as the year went on, many conditions created a fertile breeding ground for the particular strain of influenza, which would take so many lives. From a humanitarian standpoint, with the amount of devastation the world had already seen, the eruption of this pandemic must have been especially terrifying and heartbreaking for a human race that had already witnessed such extensive violence and destruction.

CHAPTER 1

The History of the Spanish Influence Of 1918

In the implacable 1918-1919 pandemic, influenza made its historical impact. It struck the end of the First World War, which from 1914-1918, claimed the lives of 10 million soldiers. A new study indicates that influenza has claimed the lives of more than 30 million citizens globally — and far less than the conflict itself. During the pandemic, more people died of flu in one year than the entire Black Death period (1347-1351), which eradicated about 30-60% of the whole of Europe. In England alone, over 225,000 people suffered from influenza between 1918 and 1919.

No other outbreak took as many lives as the 1918-1919 Spanish influenza pandemic. Worldwide, approximately 40 million citizens died, when this virulent disease reached city by city (almost 70 million deaths is estimated). There are loads of stories of individuals suffering within hours of first falling sick. The mortality risk was most significant in individuals under the age of 50 who were notably susceptible to severe influenza disease for unexplained reasons.

In early spring 1918, the first outbreaks of influenza arose in Kansas. In the spring, officials reported more reports from Europe, although this flu did not appear to be more severe than usual. In late summer, though, the virus was more lethal. Arms of diseases soon moved across towns, countries, and continents, crippling clinics, and medical staff. In the autumn of 1918, the term Spanish flu originated from the devastating effects of the flu in Spain.

There was no medication or an appropriate antidote for influenza in 1918. In reality, most scientists assumed that instead of a virus, it was bacteria-induced influenza. While several other diseases have had vaccinations, several ineffective and potentially harmful influenza vaccines have been planned, a successful influenza vaccine has been produced for decades. There were no antibiotics for the management of virulent bacterial infections that arose as a consequence of influenza.

The last Spanish influenza was seen in the late spring of 1919. The virus migrated through the 1920s into relative harmlessness and proceeded to spread for several decades. Since then, scientists have been willing to identify the 1918-19 pandemic as virus H1N1 influenza.

Why It Is Called Spanish Influence

We also learn about the 1918-1919 influenza pandemic called "The Spanish flu." The first influenza cases arose far from neutral Spain at Fort Riley Military Base in Kansas, though. Unit cook Albert G registered sick with a fever of 40oC at Fort Riley's Camp Funston on 4 March 1918. In days, 522 people registered ill, and 1,100 soldiers were admitted to the influenza hospital by the end of the month. Of these, 237 acquired pneumonia, and 38 died (approximately 20 percent). Therefore, if the pandemic started in California, then it was the "Spanish

Flu" mentioned. Historians are now arguing this misnomer, although the most plausible reason is that Spain was dying early and murdered 8 million citizens in May 1918 with a significant amount of casualties.

The Spanish flu did not originate from Mexico, but it was featured in the press. Throughout the First World War, Spain was a neutral nation with international media reporting the war from the outset and published in Madrid for the first time in late May 1918. Meanwhile, the Allied countries and the Central Powers had war censors that covered up reports of flu to preserve strong moral values. Although Spanish news outlets were the only ones that mentioned flu, many assumed that it emerged from there (the Spanish claimed that the virus came from France and named it a 'French flu').

Scientists also do not know with certainty where the Spanish flu emerged, while hypotheses point to France, China, Great Britain, or the US, where the first recorded case was registered in Fort Riley, Kansas, on March 11, 1918.

Some suspect that untreated soldiers distributed the disease around the country to other military camps and took it abroad. Throughout March 1918, 84,000 U.S. soldiers entered the Atlantic, and 118,000 more arrived the following month.

First Assessments Assessed

When the 1918 grip hit, physicians and scientists were unsure about what caused it or how it was treated. Contrary to the current situation, there were no effective vaccines or antivirals, medicines that treat influenza. Throughout America, the first approved flu vaccine was developed in the '40s. Over the following decade, suppliers of vaccinations regularly developed vaccinations that could better monitor and deter potential pandemics. It was complicated by the fact that areas of America had been left with a lack of doctors and other healthcare professionals in World War I. And many of the available U.S. medical staff came down with flu.

Clinics became so overwhelmed with grip patients in certain places that schools, private homes, and other facilities turned into change clinics.

Officials in certain cities enforced quarantines, required the residents, including schools, churches, and theatres, to wear masks and shut public spaces.

Boy Scouts in New York City, according to the NYT, confronted men they noticed smoking on the ground and issued them cards reading, "You break the sanitary code" during the pandemic.

CHAPTER 2

Socio-Economic Consequences of the World's Worst Crisis in Those Years

Economic Impact

Following contacts, executing isolates, and detaching infectious cases involve critical human asset and staffing costs. As an explosion grows, new offices may be built to deal with new contagious situations expanding interest in consumable clinical supplies, specialized defensive hardware, and medications.

Reduced government income worsens fiscal stresses brought about by expanded uses, where charge frameworks are more vulnerable, and government budgetary limitations are more extreme. Whereas reaction costs flooded, financial movement eased back, and isolates and curfews decreased government ability to gather revenue.

Collateral profitable effect of epidemic evaluated virtually through calculable general balance simulations; the exact writing is less evolved.

Proof recommends that pestilences and pandemics can have significant social and political outcomes, making conflicts among states and residents, dissolving state limit, driving population displacement, and increasing social pressure and discrimination.

The last pre-modern epidemic related to enormous socio-political change, driven by immense mortality stuns and the resulting population change. Significantly, deaths emerging from the presentation of different infections drove legitimately to the breakdown of numerous indigenous social orders and debilitated the indigenous people groups' establishments, as well as the military ability to the degree that they got powerless against European conquest.

Proof suggests that scourges and epidemics can enhance existing political strains and spark distress. The inconvenience of isolates was seen with doubt by fragments of the general population and restriction of political leaders.

Also, fear can lead to an upsurge of the "worried well" looking for extra consideration, and further troubling the social care system.

During the 2014 West Africa Ebola scourge, lack of routine care for malaria, HIV/AIDS, and tuberculosis prompted an expected 10,600 extra deaths in Guinea, Liberia, and Sierra Leone. This roundabout loss of life almost approached the 11,300 deaths directly brought about by Ebola in those countries. Also, redirection of assets, clinical assets, and staff prompted a 30 percent decline in regular youth vaccination rates in influenced countries. During the 2009 flu pandemic, a more prominent flood in emergency clinic affirmations for flu and pneumonia was related to measurably huge increments in deaths attributable from acute myocardial infarction and stroke. But, during a pandemic, recognizing which deaths are attributable from the epidemic itself, and which are merely coincidental, might be impossible.

Their capacity to give care might be reduced. At last flu, medicinal services workers may be not able to work since they are sick themselves, and need to think about sick relatives, as well as need to think about kids as a result of school closures; or they are afraid.

Patterns Affecting Pandemic Risk

A few models have influenced pandemic likelihood, readiness, and reduction. Different variables like population development, expanding urbanization, higher travel, and availability between populace focus, living space loss, environmental change, and expanded collaborations at the human-creature interface influence the probability of pandemic occasions by expanding either the likelihood of a spark occasion.

Long-Term Consequences and Memories

The influenza pandemic has had drastic long-term impacts in parts of Africa, though people do not directly talk about the disease in oral history. The epidemic in southwest Tanzania claimed maybe 10 percent of the population and resulted in the worst famine in oral history. People equate the hunger with the First World War, fought in the region from battles on the German East Africa / Nyasaland frontier in 1914 to the final pillaging before the German surrender in November 1918. As the first quotes demonstrate, people equate hunger with illness, too. Because people call various diseases, rather than influenza, it may contribute to the impression because the sickness was incidental to the famine and subsequent developments. It was, however, the peculiarity of the 1918-19 influenza (high youth morbidity and mortality rates) and its timing, both in the annual rhythm period (planting season) and in combination with social and political upheavals that led to famine and the reactions of the people.

CHAPTER 3

Self-Adjusting and Preventive Measures, Prophylaxis, Social Distance, Preventive Measures, Social Distance, Preventive Measures for People

Prophylaxis

I n 1918, the upper respiratory system was considered as the main entry gate for the causative agent. Physicians recommended the plentiful use of inhalation and nasal douches with oil, menthol, formaldehyde, hydrogen peroxide, and several other substances. Appropriate prevention, for the present-day reader, might have been the administration of Aspirin or the use of alcohol. Stranger, in fact, bizarre, appears one physician's advice of smoking; others suggested the daily usage of a black mercury ointment – which has to be applied four times a day in the nasal cavity - or to trickle silver nitrate drops into the eyes. The reason behind the latter was that the conjunctiva was considered as an entry gate of the disease as well, or at least it was not regarded as impossible.

Incomprehensible, for the present-day observer, is the usage of Isotonic Seawater, ozone therapy, or harmonic vibrations as means of cognitive therapy. One of these proposed cures was sent to the Surgeon General from an inmate of the New York State Hospital for the Insane. Not solely mentally challenged people gave strange advice; also, one physician of 40 years of practice, recommended to *"sprinkle a little sulfur in each shoe every morning"* as a proper precaution against the disease.

A cure, to ward off the flu, was desperately searched; some experimented with camphor or salted herring bags around their necks. Others drank, on the other hand, the secretion of a skunk's musk gland, stirred into a glass of water. In Switzerland, the abundant use of nicotine or snuff powder was advised. However, physicians railed against these obscure methods and told the people to see a doctor instead. One physician from Charleston, West Virginia summed it up in a letter to the editor of the American Journal of Public Health:

Nurses, doctors, hospital visitors, and those suspected of being infected by influenza were ordered to use flu masks. Minneapolis alone ordered 15,000 covers from the Red Cross on October 1, 1918. Tens of thousands of costumes were manufactured by the Northern Division of the American Red Cross. Seattle and several other American cities passed mandatory face mask ordinances. Law violators faced a $5 fine and arrest. Contemporary medicine was divided into a mask supporting party and its opponents, the latter one argued, that *"it would hardly be humane to add [a mask] to the respiratory difficulties under which"* influenza patients were suffering, and that improperly manufactured masks could not be expected to guarantee protection. Dr. J. W. Inches,

Detroit's health commissioner, was one of the critics, who declared, that *"these masks are worthless";* they seemed to such an extent porous to him that even *"a mosquito could jump through them."* For Jordan, it was confident as well, that not all flu masks in use were adequately made.

On the other hand, supporters claimed their usefulness, quoting experiments, which had shown that face masks prevent the dissemination of certain pathogenic bacteria. Despite these reasonable critics on the use of gauze masks, at least they offered some kind of solution to the droplet infection threat. Wearing masks was a common practice, by World War I, in hospital operating rooms; the usage by laypeople, however, was one of the novelties of the

Spanish Influenza pandemic. Wearing masks was considered as an emblem of public-spiritedness and discipline. Women volunteers manufactured them besides bandages and socks for the American military, and newspapers gave instructions on how to produce and wash them. Women with a unique sense of haute couture made their flu masks even out of chiffon.

Such as New York City's anti-spitting campaign from the late 1890s, the rise of public awareness was based on education, moral suasion, and police enforcement. Fines and arrests for violators had helped implement the campaign as well. Placards were posted in railway stations and other public places to inform on influenza. Boy Scouts handed out cards to people who spat on the sidewalk that read: *"You are violating the Sanitary Code."* Spatter, who was caught by law enforcement officers, were rounded up and brought to court; 134 men, for instance, were fined on October 4, 1918, with $1 at Jefferson Market Court. Violators could be technically punished for jail time, but no record exists as reference.

Chicago passed a law on the usage of handkerchiefs; people who sneezed or coughed without the use of a scarf faced possible arrest. One reason to emphasize the use of bandannas was its comfortable and easy practice; gauze masks, on the other hand, were expensive and uncomfortable to wear. However, for some weaker members of the American society, even a frequently washed handkerchief represented a luxury.

Despite the threat of being fined or even arrested, most people did not care much about these Public Health measures, even persons who should have known better violated the rules. San Francisco's major, for example, was attending, at the height of the pandemic, the Armistice Day parade, while letting his flu mask dangle on his arm. Even worse, San Francisco's Commissioner of Health was fined for not wearing his mask, while attending a boxing match. However, according to an article, which was published in *The Lancet* in March 1919, surgical gauze masks were ineffective against influenza, even the better-considered muslin fabric had to be used in at least four layers. Large-mesh gauze was found to be of no use at all, even at a thickness of ten sheets.

Tests in 1919 showed that "bacteria" could be spread up to one meter (3.3 feet) in ordinary speech, and over three meters (9.8 feet) by a cough or sneeze. Influenza is a crowd disease; from its onset, the disease was linked to troop movements, crowded places, and movie theaters.

Isolation of the sick, quarantine measurements and policies against crowding of public spaces can be considered as the most effective preventive methods in fighting the disease's spread.

In 1918, up to the present day, the only valid measure against influenza was isolation, until the virus has run its course. Numerous attempts to isolate communities were made in 1918/19, but quarantines are not practical and hard, respectively, impossible to manage. One of the quarantines that performed well was also the biggest: the quarantine of Australia, which was also the last nation or continent to experience the pandemic. The maritime quarantine lasted from October 1918 to May 1919. During that time, the government had administered 79 infected ships, which had 48,072 uninfected, 2,795 affected passengers, and 10,456 crew members on board. There was no evidence *"of a spread of infection by a demonstrable chain from person or vessel in quarantine to shore population"* throughout that period. At the same time, New Zealand and South Africa were suffering from an extremely severe form of epidemic influenza. Despite the isolation measurements on the part of the Australian government, flu appeared in mid-January 1919 in Melbourne; subsequently, the disease spread throughout Victoria and the other Australian states.

Nonetheless, isolation kept out the severe influenza virus for several months, and the supposedly weaker virus claimed fewer deaths. Australia was affected by the pandemic from January to June 1919, and the mortality rate reached a maximum of 33.5 for New South Wales and 18.7 in Victoria. Without this quarantine, Australia would have possibly suffered as severe as neighboring New Zealand. Spanish influenza made its appearance in almost every location worldwide, only the U.S. governed island of Eastern Samoa seemed to have excluded the virus, utilizing an extensive naval quarantine. On the neighboring island of Western Samoa, on the other hand, horrifying 25% of the population died. Quarantine measures worked out for some locations, but not as a general rule; the word was received that Fairbanks and Alaska, and Lake City, Colorado, escaped the flu in the United States.

For vast agglomerations, such as New York, quarantine measures were considered as not practical and anti-trade.

So to say, the economy had priority over the wellbeing of the inhabitants. On the implementation of preventive measures prevailed disagreement between the Minneapolis' health commissioner Dr. Guilford, and St. Paul's magistrate Dr. Simon. Dr. Guilford tended to be initiative and prevent possible cases, whereas Dr. Simon had a more passive understanding and tended merely towards the response to individual circumstances. The latter insisted that it would be more useful to isolate influenza patients than to close public places. The Minneapolis health commissioner, on the other hand, regarded isolation as useless to prevent the spread of the disease.

The Minnesota State Board of Health as well recommended the use of handkerchiefs to cover sneezes and coughs. The avoidance of crowds and sick persons, as well as plenty of fresh air together with consulting a physician if feeling unwell, were advised. Additionally, the Board banned all public funerals in Minnesota; solely immediate relatives of the deceased person were allowed to attend.

Darlene vividly described the situation in the central city of Brown County, New Ulm. The town was closed down, no public meetings allowed, schools closed, no church services held, mortuaries were full, and bodies buried without ceremony. Toe tags were ordered for hospital patients when they were still lying in their beds. In some communities, a shortage of coffins occurred. Because public funerals were banned, mourners walked by the deceased person's house, to see the body, that was propped up the window. Wreaths or crepes, hanging on doors, were symbolizing a family's death – black indicated middle-aged persons, grey the elderly. The Brown County Journal brought some sarcasm into the grim situation and announced the "Flu Flitter" as the new seasonal dance:

> *You take one step forward, sneeze twice, pivot and swallow two quinine capsules, swing your partner, then cough in unison, take two steps backward, and blow your noses, and waltz home and consult a doctor.*

Similar to the sometimes-bizarre seeming prophylaxis methods, the pandemic gave birth to endless new means of therapy and rediscovered old and occasionally odd, occasionally dangerous, healing practices. Home remedies as well as experienced their renaissance in the pre-antibiotic age.

CHAPTER 4

Vaccine against Influence, the Case of the Pfeiffer Vaccine

The Flu Vaccine

The vaccination of 1918 did not work individually against influenza. At the time, researchers thought the flu was caused by bacteria, and they were able to make a vaccine, but it only affected a specific pneumonia bacterium. Influenza is caused by a virus, and although the medical community knew some infectious agents were smaller than bacteria, they did not know enough yet about the nature of microorganisms to produce an effective flu vaccine.

Who Should Get a Flu Shot?

• People with asthma, or long-term diseases (such as HIV or heart disease, chronic lung disease)

• As for children, it is a parent's decision whether to give the vaccine by looking at the risk/benefit ratio for their children. The death rate in children from flu is virtually zero, while mercury can have severe effects on a developing brain.

Side Effects

- Soreness at the site of the vaccination.

- Fever, tiredness, and sore muscles.

- Serious allergic reaction if you have an egg allergy (the vaccine is grown in chicken eggs)

- Guillain-Barre syndrome: a debilitating neurological disorder

[1]Hydrotherapy for Immune Stimulation

The use of water in healing dates back to the first medical records of Hippocrates. Hydrotherapy, which means "water therapy," involves the use of hot and cold applications of water to the body. Hydrotherapy is beneficial:

- To stimulate the removal of toxins and waste

- To strengthen the digestive system

- To stimulate the immune and metabolic systems

- To improve circulation

Hydrotherapy stimulates the immune system and fights infections in two ways. It increases the amount of blood flow to specific areas of the body, and it boosts immune cells in the digestive tract and thymus gland.

Warming Body Treatment

The goal of this treatment is to artificially induce a fever by increasing the body's core temperature. It stimulates the immune system and assists in destroying heat-sensitive viruses/bacteria, as well as promoting detoxification and elimination through the skin (via sweating).

Contraindications for Warming Body Treatment

Do not use this treatment if you have any of the following conditions: severe illness or decreased vitality (elderly or very young children), pre-existing high fever, tachycardia, arrhythmia, other cardiac deficiency conditions, open wounds or active bleeding, pulmonary deficiency, respiratory insufficiency, lupus, acute high blood pressure, diabetes, pregnancy, breastfeeding, or multiple sclerosis.

Directions

1.   Make sure someone else is at home with you for the treatment duration.

2.   Immerse as much of your body as possible in the tub for five minutes.

3.   Immediately dry off, dress warmly and get into a bed or couch lined with towels or a flannel sheet, with at least two wool blankets on top.

4.   Place a hot water bottle or heating pad over the upper abdomen (over the liver, stomach, and spleen).

5.   Sweat for at least twenty minutes. Drink plenty of water during your sweat so you'll remain hydrated.

6.   After the sweat, have some broth, soup, or vegetable juice to help replenish electrolyte minerals lost during the sweating process.

7.   Make sure to dry off entirely and dress in warm, dry clothes to prevent getting chilled after the sweat.

Contrast Hydrotherapy

Contrast hydrotherapy is the application of hot and cold water to the body to boost the immune system by increasing circulation in the body and to stimulate the thymus gland. Contrast hydrotherapy can also keep you warm during cold winter days by stimulating circulation throughout the entire body. It is recommended to use during the recovery period after infection and daily during the cold winter months as a preventative measure.

Contrast hydrotherapy has been traditionally used in Sweden and Finland as part of the sauna tradition. Participants will sit in a hot sauna and then jump in a cold river. This process is repeated several times to obtain the desired results. A milder version is to end a shower with a cycle of hot and cold water.

Directions

1.   Check water heater is set to 1200F or less.

2.   Take a hot shower for at least 5 minutes.

3.   Once the body is heated, switch to the coldest water tolerable and rinse the whole body, including the torso, for at least 15-30 seconds.

4.   Switch the water to the hottest temperature for 2-3 minutes and then repeat step 2.

5.   If desired, repeat the cycle, ending with cold and then dry off. Gradually increase the length of time exposed to the virus and progressively decrease the temperature of cold water used.

Homemade Vapor Rub

Vapor rub is most effective at opening congested nasal and sinus passages, thus clearing congestion in the upper airways.

1.   Combine 20 drops of essential oils (any combination of eucalyptus, hyssop, thyme, peppermint, or basil) with two oz.—almond or olive oil.

2.   Rub the oil mixture on the chest area to relieve chest congestion or apply to a cotton ball you can sniff to open the nasal and sinus passages.

Carrot Poultice

Carrot poultice is very helpful in decreasing painful sore throats. It has outstanding results in children under six years old but also works for older children and adults. A carrot poultice can be made either hot or cold, depending on which feels best.

Contraindications

Carrot allergy or sensitivity, open wounds

Note: Do not wrap the cloth or scarf around the neck too tightly. It should be firmly against the skin but loose enough to insert a finger between the fabric and throat.

CHAPTER 5

Factors Associated with Influential Infection and Changes in Mortality in 1918, Age, Immunity Response, Genetic Differences, Malnutrition, Ground Meetings, Masks, and Hygiene

The Mortality Rate

Spanish influenza contaminated around 500 million individuals, about a fourth of the world's population.

Estimates concerning what number of tainted individuals passed on fluctuate significantly, yet this season's flu virus is, in any case, viewed as perhaps the deadliest pandemic in history. A 2005 indicator put the loss of life at most likely 50 million (under 3% of the worldwide populace), and conceivably as large as 100 million (more than 5%). However, a reassessment in 2018 assessed the aggregate to be around 17 million. However, this has been contested. With a total populace of 1.8 to 1.9 billion, these appraisals relate to somewhere in the range of 1 and 6 percent of the people. This influenza slaughtered a more significant number of individuals in 24 weeks than HIV/AIDS executed in 24 years. The Black Death, which endured any longer, murdered on a lot higher level of the world's then littler population.

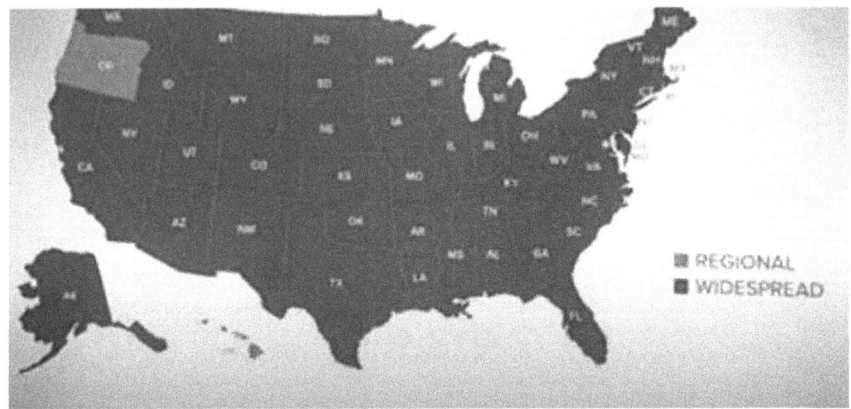

The infection was executed in numerous places in the world. Some 12-17 million individuals reportedly passed on in India, about 5% of the population. The loss of life in India's British-governed areas was 13.88 million. Arnold (2019) gauges at any rate of 12 million dead. Appraisals for the loss of life in China have changed widely, a range that mirrors the absence of incorporated assortment of wellbeing information at the time because of the Warlord time frame. The main gauge of the Chinese loss of life was made in 1991 by Patterson and Pyle, which evaluated China had a loss of life of somewhere in the range of 5 and 9 million.

Nonetheless, this 1991 examination was scrutinized by investigations because of imperfect approach, and fresher examinations have distributed evaluations of a far lower death rate in China. The lower assessments of the Chinese loss of life depend on the low death rates that were found in Chinese port-urban areas (for instance, Hong Kong) and on the suspicion that poor interchanges kept this season's cold virus from entering the inside of China. However, some contemporary paper and mail station reports, just as reports from teacher specialists, recommend that influenza penetrated the Chinese inside and that flu was terrible in certain areas in the field of China.

In Japan, 23 million individuals were infected at any rate; 390,000 announced deaths. In the Dutch Indies (presently Indonesia), 1.5 million were accepted to have died among 30 million inhabitants. And in Tahiti, 13% of the populace passed on in one month. So also, in Samoa, 22% of the number of inhabitants in 38,000 passed on inside two months. In New Zealand, this season's flu virus killed an unexpected 6,400 and 2,500 indigenous Maori in about a month and a half, with Māori died at multiple. In Iran, the mortality was exceptionally high: as indicated by a gauge, somewhere in the range of 902,400 and 2,431,000, or 8% to 22% of the all-out populace died.

In the States, approximately 27 percent of the number of inhabitants in 105 million got contaminated, and about 600,000 to 675,000 were recorded dead (0.48 to 0.64 percent of the population). Native American clans were especially hard hit. In the Four Corners zone, there were 3,293 enrolled lots of deaths among Native Americans. Also, an entire Inuit and the Alaskan Native town networks reportedly died in Alaska. In Canada, 50,000 died. In Ghana, the flu plague murdered in any event 100,000 people. In British Somaliland, one authority evaluated that 7% of the local populace died.

Patterns of Fatality

The pandemic generally killed youthful grown-ups. In (1918–1919), 99% of pandemic flu death in the U.S. happened in individuals below 65, and almost 50% of deaths were in youthful grown-ups 20 to 40 years of age.

In 1920, the death rate among individuals under 65 had diminished six-fold in no small portion of the death pace of individuals more than 65, yet 92% of deaths despite everything happened in individuals below 65. This is bizarre, since flu is regularly generally fatal to powerless people, for example, newborn children under age two, grown-ups over period 70. In 1918, more seasoned adults may have had incomplete insurance, brought about a presentation to the 1889–1890 influenza pandemic, known as the "Russian flu." As indicated by a student of history, John M. Barry, the most helpless of all – that is most likely to die of the virus– were pregnant ladies. He announced that in thirteen investigations of hospitalized ladies in the pandemic, the death range from 23% to 71%. For the pregnant ladies who endure labor, more than one-quarter (26%) lost the child. Another peculiarity was that the flare-up across the board in the midyear and fall (in the Northern Hemisphere); flu is typically more regrettable in winter. The Current investigation has demonstrated the infection to be especially savage since it triggers a cytokine storm (overcompensation of the body's insusceptible framework), which assaults the more grounded resistant arrangement of youthful adults. One gathering of analysts recuperated the infection from the collections of solidified casualties and transfected creatures with it. The animals endured quickly dynamic respiratory failure and consequent death through a cytokine storm. The reliable insusceptible responses of youthful grown-ups were hypothesized to have desolated the body. However, the more fragile resistant reactions of kids and moderately aged adults brought about fewer deaths among those groups. In quick advancing cases, the mortality was principally from pneumonia, by infection instigated aspiratory combination. More slow advancing cases included optional bacterial pneumonia, and conceivably neural inclusion that prompted mental clutters now and again. A few deaths came about because of malnourishment. An examination led by He et al. (2011) utilized an unthinking displaying way to deal with the study of the three influxes of the flu pandemic in the early 1900s. They inspected the components that underlie inconstancy in fleeting examples and their relationship to patterns of mortality and grimness. Their examination proposes that brief varieties in transmission rate give the best clarification, and the range in transmission required to create these three waves is inside organically conceivable values. Another examination by (2013) utilized a basic pestilence model fusing three variables to derive the reason for the three floods of the influenza pandemic of 1918. These variables were school opening and shutting temperature changes all through the episode, and human conduct changes in light of the flare-up. Their demonstrating results indicated that each of the three components is significant, yet human social reactions demonstrated the hugest effects. A recent report found that U.S. urban communities that actualized early and broad non-clinical measures (isolate and so on.) endured no antagonistic financial impacts.

.

CHAPTER 6

Prevention against Further Pandemic Epidemics, Possibility of a Future Epidemic

Stay Healthy

Along with particular disease prevention strategies for illnesses such as influenza, there are several activities that people can do daily to stay healthy. These include:

• Eating nutritious food

• Getting enough rest

• Having a regular exercise program

• Managing stress

• Remembering personal hygiene, especially frequent hand-washing with soap and water and covering a cough or sneeze.

The Centers for Disease Control and Prevention (CDC) you may want to read more about the different topics.

Another necessary Quarantine can be ordered by government resource about health promotion is the World Health Organization (WHO). You may also want to visit this site and read about the health promotion programs being implemented in different parts of the world.

Prevent Disease

There are also particular activities used to prevent illness from occurring. Influenza prevention activities include:

• Vaccination

• The use of antiviral medications,

• Personal hygiene (hand-washing and covering a cough with tissue),

• Voluntary "social distancing" — or staying away from large crowds, because large numbers of people may be sick, coughing and sneezing and not using personal hygiene measures.

Vaccination

Vaccination is the main activity used to prevent influenza.1 Influenza vaccines are recommended each year for individuals over the age of 6 months except those with egg allergies. Although vaccines are not 100% perfect in preventing influenza illness, they are safe and reactions, if they do occur, are usually mild. 2 3

Yearly vaccine production takes time and is affected by many complex issues, including changes in the types of viruses circulating throughout the world. If a pandemic were to occur, vaccines that protect against the specific infection causing the epidemic would not be immediately available. Research and vaccine production in a particular influenza virus would take approximately six months before a vaccine would be widely available to the general public.

Antiviral medications

Antiviral medications are also specific measures used to combat influenza. The four antiviral drugs commonly used to treat disease around the world now include rimantadine.4 In the United States, two medications have been approved by the FDA and zanamivir.5 National and state plans have priorities for dispensing antiviral drugs during a pandemic. Still, there is also concern about the ability to get medications to people within the first 24-48 hours that signs of illness appear. These medications are most effective when taken during the early stages of the disease.

Personal Hygiene

The third specific measure used for disease prevention is personal hygiene. This includes adequate hand-washing with soap and water and respiratory health. Respiratory hygiene is another way of describing using a tissue to "cover a cough or sneezing," rather than coughing into the open air.

Hand-washing: Adequate hand-washing with soap and water means washing all surfaces for at least 15 seconds.

We suggest the following steps:

- Turn on the faucet and wet your hands

- Cover the palms and the back of your hands with soap

- Scrub the palms and the end of your hands

- Scrub in between your fingers and underneath your fingernails

- Scrub for 15 seconds

- Rinse the soap off your hands and dry your hands with a towel; you can turn off the faucet using the cloth so that you do not get any germs on your clean hands from the tap.

- Wash Hands with Soap and Water for 15 Seconds

The Centers for Disease Control and Prevention (CDC) has posters and brochures that can be downloaded from its website and used in homes, businesses, and other organizations to remind people to "cover cough and sneeze," and how and when to wash hands. You can print the posters from the CDC website at:

Social Distancing

Social distancing is a term used to describe "staying away from large crowds of people" because many of them may already be sick, coughing, and sneezing. This means avoiding any large gathering or event to stay well. Avoiding crowds in entertainment facilities, shopping malls, sports events, and staying home from school and other collections may slow the spread of an infection in a community.6 Social distancing is voluntary.

Quarantine

Quarantine refers to confining people who have been exposed to a disease. It means that someone who is well but proved to a sick person is limited at home (or in a hospital) for some time. This action may prevent further transmission of disease. In past pandemics, quarantine was used to slow the spread of illness. The quarantine can be ordered by government officials and enforced by law.

CHAPTER 7

Reasons for the Expansion of an Epidemic

Influenza spread through the Military Hospital in Pittsburgh in 1918 provided a time of massive amounts of data collection, lasting about five weeks, that was extremely valuable for real-time evaluation of the components of an epidemic. It will dive into the progression of the disease how it is seen in clinics and hospitals, from early to late events, as it was known during this time. There are plenty of differences depending on the surrounding area, region, and population, which will also be appreciated to shine more light on any possible associations. These observations will be made within the context of the height of an epidemic, from individuals who died from the disease, in which there was evidence of a lung infection process. It involves 639 patients admitted to the hospital during this time, of which 35 died. All the individuals were from military camps, were enrolled in the army, and were ages 18-30 in good physical condition.

There were no consistent external characteristics that could be pointed to as a mark of influenza. Lack of oxygen (cyanosis), which turns the skin blue, was seen in the face, head, neck, and shoulders commonly, but not enough to be universal. Of these cases, it was always the upper part of the body that had this trait, with the face still being the most affected, particularly the lips and ears. It was a common sign in ordinary pneumonia as well. Some places where the lack of oxygen was also evident were the fingertips under the nails, more so in the upper extremities than the lower. There was no evidence of swelling that came with this. One patient had a rash on the chest, which looked like pinpoint purplish dots. There were occasional skin lesions that seemed to be the start of boils or pustules, which were common post-influenza symptoms. It was thought that this could indicate the presence of influenza in the surrounding tissues.

There were two cases where there were burst blood vessels in the eyes. They were both limited to one eye. One example also had yellowing of the eye and skin: a symptom commonly seen in liver damage. This patient had corresponding liver damage.

There were no kidney issues with any of the patients. Interestingly, in the 1890 epidemic in Canada, there was substantial kidney damage. These individuals also had swelling, which was not present in the Pittsburgh subjects. Swelling is a known sign of kidney damage, which is worth note.

The majority of individuals had few visible lesions in the nose, mouth, or throat. Some had complained of throat dryness before death, but there were no evident causes of this. Congestion of the trunk was much milder than similar respiratory diseases, but the bleeding was still common during the acute illness. Causes of nose bleed were not found, and it was thought to be unusual the lack of running noses in the population. Also, while some patients complained of hoarseness, which was then found to be caused by swelling of the larynx (voice box), this finding was not consistent. It was below the vocal cords that the real evidence of a respiratory illness began.

Additional features of the trachea inflammation included backed up blood vessels and hemorrhaging, stretching of spaces in between tissues, and local swelling limited to this region. It led to damage to the lining of the trachea, as all the contents leaked out into the area. In the patients autopsied, this process seemed further along, with larger areas of damage to the lining. It led to swelling of the inner portions of the trachea. Damaging processes occurred to nearby cities as blood vessels and cells leaked their contents. However, interestingly, there were still very few areas of dead tissue. Blood clots were common in the small blood vessels of the city, indicating a distinct characteristic of this illness. I was also suspected to be the case in the lower regions of the lung, which would make breathing more difficult.

Another change demonstrated in this area was about the lymphatic system, which controls the drainage of all waste made by cells and is a route for immune cells to follow. These channels typically were found to be enlarged with fluid, and with immune cells called lymphocytes. It is usually a response to an invasion.

The amount and characteristics of the thin film lining the trachea were correlated to the extent of the illness. Underneath this layer and the lining of the trachea, differences in injury could also be observed to determine disease severity. The mucus glands seemed to have no role in the inflammatory process, which may be due to over secretion and subsequent protection from invasion. It could be partly how the lung protects itself.

The lesions seen in the bronchi, which are the continuations of the trachea into each lung, were very much a continuation of the findings observed in the trachea. The amount of inflammation seen in the trachea is very comparable to that in the upper airway. As the track progresses downward, these findings generally become milder, and it was thought that the change in material facilitated this (lower airway is more composed of muscle, versus cartilage, with more lymphatic drainage).

The recovery process of these parts of the lung was challenging to observe since the patients never recovered from illness. There was some evidence that the body attempted to repair damaged areas with connective tissue. The amount of connective tissue made in some instances could have restricted airflow to that area of the lung, which would cause shortness of breath to the individual. It was assumed that those individuals who recovered without loss of lung function preserved enough of their healthy lung tissue to regenerate it in the usual way that the lung replaces cells. In the few cases where patients were autopsied outside of this study after they had overcome influenza, the lungs appeared normal 5-6 weeks following resolution.

The progression of influenza-pneumonia was able to be elicited from the data. The earliest sign was congestion, followed by swelling, small bleeding, and immune system involvement. At this point, the tissue would start to heal or become overwhelmed and die. Most cases where the patient died did so during the first three stages, evident by the lack of any lung healing. Surprisingly, a large proportion of these died during the early stage, which would be unusual in other lung injuries. It was difficult to determine how long this process would take, as, in influenza, the step where the lung was congested was very variable. Using the start of the illness, however, it was suggested that the progression took somewhere around five days. Of note, the amount of lung volume involved was often not enough to compromise the amount of air a person could get to induce death, meaning that there must have been an acute process contributing to this not evident at autopsy.

The lack of distribution to one or two lobes of the lung is a logical reason why the physical exam findings were challenging to elucidate in influenza. Typically, in pneumonia, when one entire portion is in recovery and not functioning, that changes the breath sounds that can be heard with a stethoscope. When this recovery is not uniform, there is enough breath that seems to complicate the findings, to the point where it could be missed on physical exam that a portion of a lung is affected.

The summary of all of these effects on the lung is that, unfortunately, the impact of influenza pneumonia is both complex and inconsistent. Resolution may be quick and more efficient than could be observed if there was no damage to the lining or may be delayed if the immune system became involved. It commonly affects the areas of the lung in an unpredictable pattern and is often gone as quickly as it came, leaving a potential site for secondary infection. The majority of cases seems to experience complete healing or a minor amount of scarring, but if persistent, can end up with a complicated illness. Those who start to recover before the invasion of the immune system begin tended to have the best outcome.

CHAPTER 8

Recent Assumptions about the Origin of the Spanish flu

T he geographical origin of the Spanish is still the subject of controversy today. Influenza viruses are continually transforming, mixing genetic characteristics, to escape the immune system of the hosts they infect. From year to year, there are small variations that make it necessary to create new vaccines; from time to time, the change is more radical, making the virus unrecognizable, so much that it takes the body's defenses entirely by surprise. It is in these cases that a new pandemic strain emerges. The historian Alfred W. Crosby claims that the flu originated in the American state of Kansas, the famous writer John Barry points to Haskell County as the starting point of the outbreak.

Notable is the research work carried out in 1999 by a British group led by the virologist John Oxford of St Bartholomew's Hospital and the Royal London Hospital. They identified the center of the 1918 influenza pandemic in the military camp and hospital of France, while the virus was found at the end of the 20th century in the frozen remains of a victim in the ice of Alaska. At the end of 1917, military pathologists reported the onset of a new disease, characterized by high mortality, which they recognized as "The flu." As we can easily imagine, the military hospitals of that time were overcrowded, busy treating thousands of soldiers who were victims of chemical attacks and other war wounds. They were an ideal place for the spread of a respiratory virus: about 100,000 soldiers passed through them every day.

There are, however, several other hypotheses as to the origin of the epidemic. Some have speculated that the flu originated in East Asia.

In 2014 a study of Mark Humphries of some recently discovered documents suggested that the origin of the pandemic may have been one of the collateral events of the war, the mobilization of 96 000 Chinese workers called to serve behind the British and French lines on the Western Front.

Humphries found archival evidence of a respiratory disease that would affect northern China in November 1917 and that the following year was deemed identical to "Spanish" by Chinese health officials.

The Journal of the Chinese Medical Association stated that there was insufficient evidence of virus transmission through Chinese soldiers and workers in Europe, but the contrary evidence of virus circulation within European armies already months and perhaps years before the outbreak of the 1918 pandemic.

In 1918, there was no internet, there were no social networks, but they need to find an explanation for an event that afflicts us was the same then as now. It was the same willingness to attribute our evils to an enemy, real or imaginary, struggling to accept that they come instead from that nature that we insist on always considering benign, ignoring its pitfalls.

Aspirin

Some buffaloes can, in turn, hide a core of truth. The experts do not exclude that the drug, one of the few remedies at that time available to combat high fever and headaches typical of the disease, may have contributed to an increase in some contexts the burden of the victims. While today, it is recommended not to exceed 3-4 grams per day, the US authorities recommended dosages of up to 30 grams per day.

The drug, however, was available to a few, and the mortality rate was no less where there were no drugs: one can certainly not blame the doctors' attempts at such a massacre.

Other fake news circulated regarding the hypothesis that the disease was nothing more than a biological weapon put into circulation by the enemy. From the port of Boston, where the plague was believed to have spread to the United States, a woman swore that she had seen a toxic cloud rise from a disguised German ship. In contrast, others suspected that enemy agents had disembarked from U-boats, entered the roadstead at night, and had spread the contents of vials containing the germ in cinemas, theatres, and other places frequented.

War censorship or not, we interpret the news as we want to explain it, confirming what we want to hear. And that the little virus that is cured with milk and honey may be worse than the plague, or that it may reoccur, and find us unprepared, this we do not want to hear.

The definitive proof, beyond any laboratory confirmation, came when one of the insiders (For the story Charles Stuart-Harris) fell ill with influenza after an infected ferret had sneezed in his face.

This influenza virus was referred to as "Type a," while the one discovered in 1940 in the United States by Francis was referred to as "type B." Taylor isolated type C in 1950. In the following decade, each of the researchers who had participated in the discovery of the influenza virus tried to develop an efficient vaccine against the disease.

So, in 1943 Francis, assisted by Davenport and Salk, created a vaccine on behalf of the U.S. military based on A and B virus inactivated with formalin: controlled studies on recruits exposed to the infection showed that the vaccine inoculated subcutaneously had protected 75% of subjects during a sudden outbreak of influenza type A

In 1947, the A1 appeared for the first time, and it was the beginning of the three best-known variations for type A, against which the vaccines available at the time were unpredictably wholly ineffective. In 1957 and 1968, the strains that were responsible for Asian and Hong Kong flu appeared (The names were concerning the areas where the first cases were reported). Still, already in 1948, the World Influenza Center was established in London with the precise task of monitoring variations in the influenza virus and adapting the strains to be used in the vaccine accordingly.

CHAPTER 9

Dealing with Self-Isolation

Things you can do during self-isolation that will bring you more control and satisfaction in your life;

The first thing you can do is focus on your health.

You can focus on your health. And this is extremely important because if you're not in top shape that if you do. And we hope that no one gets it. If you do contract the Pandemic, you will be able to fight it off.

Health

We can focus on exercising, and we can focus on our diet. By making sure that when we are going grocery shopping when we are stocking up, concentrate on foods that will make us healthy, that will make us energized and focusing on exercising so we can build a robust immune system, we can focus on our health.

If you're afraid of the PANDEMIC, then take care of your health because if you do contract it, then at least your body can fight it off.

Yes, there might be some time for some periods.

You'll get the symptoms, but if you can fight it off and that's a better place to be.

Projects

Let's say you always want to start a business.

You can do that now.

Let's say you want to go back and get some training.

You can do that.

Relationships

If you're living alone, then there's only so much you can do.

But if you're living with your spouse with your kids with your family members with your siblings with your parents, then you can improve those relationships you can get to know them more.

You can talk with them.

You can play games with them.

You can do more activities with them internally to build some of those relationships.

Because of the busy lives we live in, we don't get much chance to be with the ones we love the most.

Take their moment and build those relationships, the thing you can focus on.

And this is not a specific area but what you can do is you can clean up any messes.

Now what I mean by that there is not that you clean your house.

That's something you might want to do.

But what I mean by that there are probably projects that you've started that haven't been completed.

There are things on your To-Do list that you started, but you didn't finish.

There are people that you want to reach out to that you haven't reached out.

Some obligations promises need to be fulfilled.

It is a good time while you are by yourself while you do have some time.

If you're not commuting and even if you're working at home, chances are you're saving that one album or two hours on the road to focus on some of these things.

These are just some of the ideas that were there to help with this project with this education and business relationships or just cleaning up any messes.

Habits

It is a time to develop some new habits, whether it is with your health, whether it is with your business, whether it is with your education, whether you know something you just want to do, it's a hobby.

If you want to start reading now every single day, you want to start writing now. If there's something that you've been thinking about picking up, whether it's a skill like playing an instrument, you can start doing that now too.

Think about these things you can do during this time.

Just focus on what you might find that all of these are all whelming.

But if you can just focus on one and over the 10 20 days 30 days or however long you know we are asked to be in a position of self-isolation, then coming out of it, you would have done something different.

You would have done more in your life.

Focus on this, and hopefully, that should give you some guidance on what to do instead of feeling helpless and instead of feeling the anxiety but rather being in a position of control and motivation and being passionate.

CHAPTER 10

The War and Virus That Changed World

Hardly would you see anybody that'll be grateful and crave for more of either the First World War (1914-1918) or the Spanish flu of 1918. These are bitter experiences that no one would love to have again. However, there's some good in evil and evil in good. From a positive point of view, you could see that humanity has some gains alongside the pains of the war and the flu.

Nationalism and Scientific Achievements

In a desperate search for the protection from the enemy onslaught and the threat of the following flu, nationalism became the dominant attitude. Thus, the acceptance of governmental authorities was automatic. Whatever government thought was good for the citizens was readily accepted, democracy or no democracy.

So, the public health department officials had a great opportunity to step in and impose restrictive measures such as stay-at-home and social distancing at it is during the current pandemic. The war highlights the clear difference between politics or governance skills and health management skills. Armed with the new germ theories, scientists became the new bride for governments.

The good resulting from all this is that since the outbreak of WW1 and the Spanish flu, a lot of new grounds have been broken in virology research. The world has known a lot more about antiseptic surgery. We now know about vaccines to reduce the mortalities of battle wounds and the fatality of viral diseases.

These technologies are not being deployed only for those on the front, but for the benefit of everyone considered the most vulnerable. Governments naturally warmed themselves into the heart of the citizenry courtesy, these initiatives and conditions created by World War I. The prevailing social attitudes and ideas result in a relatively calm response from the public and general application of scientific concepts.

People readily succumb to restriction of movement and loss of freedom during a pandemic because it was essential for their survival, and they just have to place the needs of their nations above their own. Health officials have no other choice than to give their new allegiance to science and society. To meet with the demand to up their antes in a bid to uplift their organizations, medical and scientific communities start developing new theories that applied to the diagnosis, prevention, and treatment of influenza patients.

These and many other experiences of those times have been the stepping stones upon which the efforts to curb recent epidemics are based.

Understanding of Infectious Diseases

The time the pandemic struck was a blessing disguise. That pandemic was critical to the knowledge of the nature of infectious diseases. Up till the late 19th century, most people considered epidemics acts of gods and were approaching it unscientifically. Throughout the middle-ages, religious rites and gambles were used to address the issue. Africans and Asians were quick to appease gods and ancestors in fetish rites.

It was around the 17th century that bacteria were first observed. But the connection between them and human illnesses couldn't be understood then. In the mid-19th century, French biologist Louis Pasteur examined and explained this relationship between microorganisms and infectious diseases. Toward the end of that century, German microbiologist Robert Koch continued where Pasteur stopped and discovered more about infectious diseases.

But there was no pandemic to be used to prove their theories in many nations. When the Spanish flu broke out, scientists had the opportunity to show all they knew about disease control and management. Though they failed due to several factors, they were able to see the room for improvement.

Further application of the germ theory in the 20th century, together with improvements in hygiene, sanitation, and vaccination as a result of the lesson learned from the world war against the Spanish flu, significantly reduced fatality from the so-called 'crowd' diseases. Even though several communities sprung up as a result of the industrial revolution, no other disease has claimed and will ever claim as many lives as requested by the 1918 flu.

Yes, the 19th century, from the beginning to the end, saw many urbanites being lost to diseases such as cholera, tuberculosis, and typhus. But now, a better understanding of infectious diseases got from fighting the waves of the Spanish flu has taught the world how to control and halt them.

The world now appreciates regular washing of hands, the use of nose masks and hand gloves, avoiding crowding up in times of epidemic.

Better Understanding of Virus Nature

Specifically speaking, the world knows that virus causes flu, and it is more challenging. In an attempt to explain the arrival of the 1918 influenza pandemic, more needed to be learned about viruses.

By piecing the pandemic virus together with nucleic acid, more is discovered about the molecular nature of the pandemic virus. Examinations were carried out on the nucleic acid of viral fragments taken from pathology specimens and from bodies exhumed from the Alaskan permafrost, where whole villages were wiped out by the Spanish flu. What is the result?

Scientists discovered that the Spanish flu has some gene segments bearing semblance to those from pig and bird influenza. Oh! No wonder why it was strange to humans in 1918. But then, there was a puzzle; developed up to the level the virus can't spread among humans. So why did it spread quickly within the human population?

The answer lies, again, in consideration of wartime conditions. Living near, even after being infected, helped to transmit the virus that otherwise would run their course out in a few carriers. But as the number of the infected grew, the number of infections transmitted also grew.

With the overall increase in the size of the viral population, the stage was set for the emergence of new mutations. These found breeding grounds in some parts of human bodies and readily spread with greater ease among human carriers. Even when such rapidly spreading variants quickly out-compete the slower-growing strains of forms, more deadly strains were equally capable of being produced.

We now know that viruses that ordinary were not deadly can be transmitted from animals to humans and grow to become an even more significant threat of viral loads that are capable of overwhelming the human immune system. Several of them had come after the Spanish flu, but this understanding has helped deal with them and reducing severe illness and death. It even serves as a caution to human society to avoid practices that can quickly introduce any such pandemic.

Confined to History but Still Haunts

November 11, 1918, was a joyous day worldwide. People were rejoicing as they learned that the last shot of that pointless war had been fired. As they were embracing one another, they didn't know that they were yet to overcome the enemy that had no battlefield. They were hatching its third wave. Well, we know when the war ended, but exactly when did the Spanish virus flu end? This, again, is one of the unknown facts about influenza.

Some historians believe that the third strain ended in 1919, while a few thought that it lingered longer, claiming lives through 1920. The positive thing, however, is that never again has this deadly strain of the flu be found among humans. It never came back.

It's so puzzling that the flu virus could be forgotten so quickly to this day. Yet, each time the world witnesses a flu attack, the Spanish flu experience is always experimental in how to approach it. The recent virus flu reminds the scientists of the Spanish flu. Even though gone, scientists will continue in their research to learn about the 1918 flu to permanently halt and prevent another worldwide pandemic of virus flu.

CHAPTER 11

What Was the State of Medicine and Infectious Disease In 1918?

In Josie's day, kids didn't have to worry quite as much about the disease as her parents would have when they were children. Medicine had made significant advances in the years leading up to 1918. Josie would have been vaccinated against smallpox. Improvements in public sanitation would have helped control fatal diseases like typhoid and cholera. Although there was no vaccine to prevent diphtheria, researchers had developed an anti-toxin to fight the illness. Death rates were down for tuberculosis. Thanks to pasteurization of milk, fewer babies died from diarrhea during infancy. Still, measles and polio were a significant health threat, and the antibiotics that would help pneumonia patients would not be available until the 1930s. Influenza was only dangerous to the very young or the very old.

What was the Clean Plate Club?

The Clean Plate Club was started in 1917 to help children eat all the food on their plates and not waste it. Food was needed to feed soldiers and starving people in Europe. Because of the war, men who used to farm and raise livestock were now in the military. Farmlands of France and Belgium became battlefields. Horses that once pulled plows and farm wagons soon pulled great guns across the same fields. Women, children, and the old did what they could, even pulling plows of themselves. With half the workforce in the trenches, there were fewer people to work the farms, so there was not enough food.

Under the direction of Herbert Hoover, the United States Food Administration successfully appealed to Americans' patriotism, and our country saved sugar, fats, meat, and wheat to help feed the military and our allies. Like their French sisters, women in America stepped up to keep farms running while soldiers were away. Other folks grew food in small vegetable gardens in their back yards. Children tended gardens at school. Americans on the home front came through, saving 15 percent of our food to feed those in need.

How many people were affected by Spanish influenza, and how many died?

Experts think that some twenty-five million Americans had Spanish influenza in the ten months between September 1918 and June of 1919. That works out to one in four Americans stricken with the deadly flu. An estimated 675,000 Americans died. Worldwide estimated deaths from the flu that year, ranging from twenty million to over one hundred million. It is hard to know the exact numbers because, at the time, doctors were not required to report deaths from influenza (although this would change quickly), and in some places, health authorities were so overwhelmed they couldn't keep up with the paperwork. But significant numbers are hard to think. Maybe the lack of coffins tells the story.

So many people died in September and October of 1918 that in many cities and towns, there were not enough coffins to bury the dead, and gravediggers could not keep up. In some instances, convicts dug graves. In Philadelphia, the city morgue could handle thirty-six bodies at one time. During the epidemic, several hundred bodies were stacked in the morgue's hallways, where the decomposing corpses—neither embalmed nor on ice—waited to create their health hazard.

Influenza is a yearly occurrence. Today we call it seasonal flu. So, the disease in the winter and spring of 1918 would not be remarkable. Even the flu among soldiers in army camps would not be unusual. Soldiers unwittingly took the disease with them to other army camps on their way to France. They called the flu "three-day fever." Elsewhere the flu became known as Spanish influenza, probably because early reports of flu came from Spain, which was not censoring newspapers. By August, typically the lowest month for flu cases, a disease in Europe was deadly. Soldiers died from lung failure. Battle plans on both sides had to be altered because so many men were on sick call. Flu was a new kind of killer.

CHAPTER 12

Between the Spanish Flu 1918 and Convid19 Assessment

Major Disasters; for many people around the world, the COVID-19 pandemic is the first health crisis of their lives - but not for Montana. 1918 Late - World War I end, but more severe disaster occurs.

From January 1918 to December 1920, a Spanish pandemic killed about 50 million people worldwide. The flu killed over half a million people in the United States. Montana has lost about five thousand people to one of the highest mortality rates in the country.

It is not clear where the 1918 virus came from, but it is commonly called the Spanish flu after the Spanish and French crossings. During World War I, Spain was neutral and did not censor information. The first cases of the Spanish bombing occurred in military camps and cities in the Midwest and were quickly spread to the rest of the country.

One of the main differences between the coronavirus and Spanish influenza is that COVID-19 is primarily aimed at older men and those with immune systems, but the Spanish flu targeted healthy-looking men. Mullen wrote and published articles on the Spanish flu crisis in Montana and published the report in March 2008. In 1918, he introduced the CNN to the science behind the high death rates for men. News explained, the flu multiplies on getting to the respiratory tracks, they released the so-called 'cytokine storm.' In other words, your solid immune cells are filled with a lot of occlusion and dead cells. A person in edible physical shape leaves at 7:30 a.m. to work in at the break of day and pass away by 5:30 p.m."

At the beginning of the 19th century, Montana was particularly struck by the influx of young families who had moved to a prosperous state. Lack of international relations and war censorship - There were no warnings for the 1918 pandemic. It was too late. And people thought that if the leaders ordered to close shops, bars, and churches, they would die at twelve every day.

Shops were at the core of every neighborhood, so they refused to close. Not just because they lost their income, but because their area was too dependent on them," they had virtually nothing," according to Mullen. And there was a terrible complaint about the closure. And that was at the local level. The state is not closed, and your local mayor and city council do not have it organized.

The fear in 2020 is that the coronavirus will dominate the American medical system. It was the case in 1918 when insufficient to treat a large number of patients admitted to minimal health care facilities. There were no significant hospitals that we know. There are usually two or three-story buildings.

Strategies and Lessons from the 1918 Spanish Flu Epidemic

We then need to take a closer look at the Spanish epidemic of 1918 and record today's COVID-19 epidemic. Without saying a word, the Spanish flu destroyed the world and one-third of the world's population. Although science was not as advanced as it is today, there was no electronic microscopy or genetic engineering to identify the virus. Also, there is still debate as to whether the epidemic comes from Spain. It is believed that the spread of the virus after World War II expanded to millions of soldiers traveling around the world. Due to the limited space and capacity, the hospitals were overcrowded.

CHAPTER 13

False Hopes and Rumors

False Hopes

I n 1918, for a person suffering from influenza, or almost any other disease, and their families, there were a host of patent medicines advertising the healing powers of their potions. Patent medicines were a boon for those who sold and marketed them and provided false hopes for their customers. "The sick often seek the advertising doctor and believe the false assertions of the patent medicine label because they have found the medical practitioners with whom they have come in contact so incapable, so inefficient, or so exorbitant in fees that help seemed impossible at their hands."

Influenza did not care about any of the patent medicines that its victim chose to take. The first vaccine for flu was not developed until 1945, coincidentally about the same time that penicillin became available. The cause of the virus – its etiology – was not understood until 1933.

The Food and Drug Administration today has a host of laws and regulations that prevent harmful medicines from getting to market. At the time of the Spanish Influenza, though, those laws and regulations were in their nascent stage of existence.

Many patent medicines producers were out of business as a result of the new law. Others labeled their "medicines" appropriately and continued to sell their wares. Still, others ignored the law and continued to sell their cures, laced with addictive drugs, or in some cases, poisons.

The notion that there was no cure for influenza in 1918 struck some as unusual. Somehow, it was believed, the medical community was incompetent in not finding a cure for sicknesses such as the common cold. So, when a quack placed an ad claiming to have a treatment for influenza or to mitigate its effects, many people willingly believed that the impossible was possible. Spanish Influenza made people desperate to find anything that could claim to cure them or their loved ones of this dreaded disease.

It was desperate and incurable that particularly attracted the quacks to ply their trade. "The ideal patron, viewed in the light of profitable business, is the victim of some slow and wasting ailment in which recurrent hope inspires to repeat experiments with any cure that offers."

The situation was not helped when manufacturers of patent medicines made disparaging remarks regarding the medical community. "Catarrh, we are told, in its chronic form (and the complaints arising from it) is a malady which has not, up to the present time, received that attention and research from the medical faculty which it deserves." Read – doctors and researchers do not care about your suffering enough to do anything about it.

Manufacturers of these patent medicines often ran ads that appeared to be more like a news story, thereby providing unwarranted credibility to its claims. A cursory examination of patent medicines advertised in 1918 will give the reader a sense of the kinds of deceptive claims made by practitioners of deception. The reader should know that ads like these ran in many newspapers, including those in the Wyoming Valley.

The active ingredients for Hill's Cascara were as follows: cascara (a laxative), quinine sulfate, (another laxative), aspirin, and ephedrine sulfate. Though the concoction likely allowed influenza suffers from having smoother bowel movements, it did nothing to ease the symptoms of flu. Hill's was far from the only patent medicine promising relief from influenza, though.

Father John's Medicine ran an ad, running under the banner of an article titled "Victims of Influenza." To all appearances, it appeared the same as any other newsworthy story. To those willing to believe, it was yet another provider of false hope. The active ingredient in Father John's Medicine was cod liver oil. Again, there was no known connection between the consumption of cod liver oil and influenza relief.

Dr. William's Little Pink Pills for Pale People guaranteed patients would feel its soothing effects "as soon as the revitalized blood courses through the system." The Little Pink Pills held the promise that color would return to the cheeks and that appetite and digestion would return to normal. In truth, the pills contained nothing that could help those suffering from influenza – ferrous sulfate, potassium carbonate, magnesia, powdered licorice, and sugar.

Munnion's Paw Pills guaranteed to cure its customers of rheumatism, nerve problems, dyspepsia, kidney problems, and the flu. It also claimed to prevent pneumonia. Who wouldn't want a cure-all that cost only 25 cents? No need for expensive visits to a doctor – Munnion's offered a 'more gentle and humane treatment."

Upon closer examination, Munnion's Paw Pills were nothing but a fraud. The tablets contained 1.87 grains of sodium bicarbonate (baking soda); 1.81 grains of sodium chloride (table salt); 2.2 grains of Borax (useful as an ingredient in laundry soap, and fire-retardant); a trace of Phenol (a poison that causes chemical burns); and 0.12 grains of the gum (used to make chewing gum). Not one of these ingredients has any medicinal use related to the treatment of influenza, with one being a known poison.

Laxative Quinine claimed to be a world-famous cure for the grip and used by every civilized nation. While reducing malaria induced fever was a known medicinal use for quinine as early as the 17th century, there is no known correlation between the use of quinine and the easing of influenza symptoms.

Of all the excesses of the patent medicine industry, the worst were those who plied their trade by passing themselves off as legitimate doctors.

One such quack was Dr. M. Cook, who hawked three different patent medicines in one article in the Fulton County News.

The first, Pleasant Purgative Pellets were meant to ward off an attack of influenza by cleansing the bowels. The pills turned out to be nothing more than a common laxative repackaged as "pellets."

The article suggested flushing the kidneys with tablets. What this had to do with relief from influenza is anyone's guess. These tablets contained traces of acetate, carbonate, chloride, iodide, quinine, and sugar.

Finally, Dr. M. Cook suggested taking Dr. Pierce's Golden Medical Discovery to help build one's system back to a healthy state. Again, the capability of the active ingredients to bring one back to good health is questionable at best. The elixir contained water, goldenseal root, borate of soda, queen's root, black cherry bark, bloodroot, and mandrake root. Incredibly, these fake cures were sold for over ninety-one years before finally leaving the marketplace for good in the 1940s.

If placed in the same desperate straits as those who contracted Spanish Influenza, how many of us would have turned to patent medicines when all hope seemed lost? Today it seems ludicrous to think that people would fall for such hoaxes – though inevitably, we still do. The consumer was not as well educated or as well-informed in 1918.

Rumors

GERMANS CARRIED DISEASE TO U.S. So, ran a story that hit page one of many U.S. newspapers on September 20, 1918, including the Scranton Republican. Lieutenant Philip S. Doan, the director of the Health and Sanitation of the Shipping Board, was quoted as saying, "it is quite started by Huns sent ashore from German submarine boats."

The sentiment that the Germans were responsible for inflicting influenza in the world was also shared by Dr. Gordon Henry Hirschberg. Dr. Hirschberg shared his wisdom on the origination of flu in an article in the October 6 edition of the Washington Times. Hirschberg wrote, "It should be said that the term 'Spanish Influenza' is an error, for investigation proves that the disease originated in the German trenches." The doctor cited no sources for his information.

He further claimed that sailors aboard German U-Boats furthered the spread of influenza by coming ashore on U.S. soil. Perhaps Hirschberg had read Philip Doan's published statements and was merely repeating them for his use. Again, he offered no proof to substantiate his claims.

In Chicago, City Health Director J.S. McBride explained a temporary lull in cases of influenza in October 1918 by stating that "millions of influenza germs were robbed of a chance to harm Wednesday when a drenching rain washed them from the atmosphere and hurried them from their lodging places on ledges, sidewalks, and streets into the choking gutters." Nevertheless, that same day, 139 new cases of influenza were reported by area hospitals with nineteen deaths attributed to pneumonia.

Also, in Chicago, Dr. Louis Pint, a bacteriologist at the University of Chicago, believed he found the germ responsible for Spanish Influenza. He told an audience at the Chicago Medical Society "the regulation diphtheria anti-toxin is an absolute specific for the disease. Pint also claimed that he successfully treated 75 cases with the diphtheria anti-toxin and that all had recovered from influenza. This was purely coincidental, as there was (and still is) no connection between the diphtheria vaccine and a cure for flu.

These rumors and falsehoods did nothing to stem the advance of Spanish Influenza. Instead, they provided straightforward answers to a public desperate for a solution to the pandemic.

CHAPTER 14

Could There Be Another Pandemic? Are We Prepared? What "Weapons" Do We Have Against Flu Now?

Influenza pandemics occur when a new or "novel" form of the influenza virus appears. Typically, this happens several times every hundred years. In Josie's lifetime, she would have experienced not only the 1918 flu pandemic, but also the Asian flu in 1957, the Hong Kong Flu in 1968, and a swine flu scare in 1976. The 1976 scare started when soldiers at Fort Dix, New Jersey, came down with a new flu virus. Mysteriously and fortunately, that flu did not get out into the general population. Still, the disease at Fort Dix, the Camp Dix of our story, brought back fearful memories of the 1918 pandemic.

Today public health officials have plans in place to help control the spread of a future pandemic. Worldwide, governments and organizations like the Centers for Disease Control and Prevention and the World Health Organization work together to watch for potential influenza outbreaks. Their plans include identifying a latent pandemic virus as early as possible, creating a vaccine against the virus, and getting that vaccine into production. Making the vaccine takes time, and the medical community is working on ways to speed up the process to get the vaccine ready in time to protect everyone. In the meantime, we have antiviral medications that can stop or slow down viruses once a person is sick. We also have antibiotics that can treat subsequent pneumonia associated with influenza. And yes, some of the precautions used by Josie and her family in 1918 are still worth implementing: Stay home if you have the flu, cover coughs and sneezes, and wash your hands after being in public or around a sick person.

How fast did the disease spread?

During August of 1918, there were scattered reports of influenza arriving on ships docking in New York Harbor, but officials did not think much of it. As Josie and her family got ready for Labor Day and the start of school, sailors coming back from France fell ill at Boston's Commonwealth Pier. By mid-September flu was epidemic along the Eastern Seaboard, and the United States Public Health Service began issuing advice via newspapers on how to avoid catching influenza and how to treat it. By the beginning of October, Spanish flu had struck in every state in the nation. The worst weeks were in October and the first week of November. Spanish influenza slowly wound down but continued well into the winter and spring of 1919.

How did kids earn money in 1918?

Nineteen eighteen was a time when Progressive reformers were trying to control child labor, particularly for children working in factories and coal mines? One way was to make school compulsory. But kids still worked. Some worked because their families needed the money. Others worked at odd jobs to earn pocket change. Like Josie, children often worked in their parents' businesses. Kids collected bottles to make the refund money. Ten bottles might earn you ten cents, which would buy two nickel sodas or two Hershey Bars. Kids could earn money running errands, raking leaves, cutting lawns, shoveling snow. Delivering newspapers was a common way for kids to make money. Josie might have made a penny a paper. If she gave twenty-five papers a day, she'd have twenty-five cents. In a week, she could earn up to $1.75. In two to three weeks, she'd have enough to buy the middy blouse in the store, buy some Thrift Stamps, and pay for ice cream at Van Druse n's Drug Store on the way home from the library.

In 1918 goods and services were much less expensive than they are today. A dress "on-sale" for Josie would have been between $1.00 and $3.00. A coat could cost as much as $6.50. Girls' high-cut school shoes could be purchased for under $4.00.

Food and grocery items cost far less than they do today as well. But it was all relative. Wages were lower too. For example, a cup of coffee in Winslow's Drug Store might be a nickel. Campbell's soup was ten cents a can. Peanut butter was twenty-five cents for a large jar. Gum came in packages of five sticks for a nickel, but the glue was hard to get because most gums were purchased by the government for soldiers and sailors.

CHAPTER 15

Search for A Cure

By some miracle, Nixon, his wife, and little daughter did not become ill, although they were exposed to the flu every day. He took no precautions, accepting the risk as doctors do without thinking about it. What would happen to his patients if he got sick never entered his mind because he expected to take care of them? He pushed himself to the limit of his endurance, and exhaustion should have made him easy prey for illness, but neither he nor Bea became sick. It was a blessing, and Nixon had no reason for it. They were both born in 1890, so the immunity could not be attributed to illness acquired in the flu epidemic of 1889-90. It defied explanation.

New cases of the flu kept cropping up every day, and with no seeming end to the epidemic. Some disgruntled suffering people lashed out at Nixon and accused him of having some magic preventive medicine that he kept for himself and was holding out on them. The accusation was both absurd and unfair, but Nixon knew that no argument would convince these desperate people that he was playing fair with them. He simply had to live with the criticism and not let it bother him.

Revere was not alone with people clamoring for the medicine to combat this illness. The influenza virus was unknown to scientists in 1918. From the time of Hippocrates until the nineteenth century, for a span of more than two thousand years, medicine had remained virtually unchanged. Doctors did not probe beyond their observations and reasoning. When medicine began to use objective measurements and mathematics combined with the use of microscopes and scientific experiments, the practice of medicine began to change. Germany became a leader in the scientific community. European medical schools were subsidized by the state and could afford to give students rigorous scientific training while American schools without outside support did not have that luxury. America lagged woefully far behind, and scientists from the United States often traveled to Europe to study.

By the Civil War, America began to advance, however slowly. As late as 1900, many U.S. medical schools would accept any man-but, not woman-who paid tuition. Standards were shallow at most medical schools, and only one required a college degree for admission. A high school diploma sufficed for most.

Then, in 1873, John Hopkins died and left a trust to found a university and a hospital. The university opened its doors first and, not until twenty years, in 1893, did the Johns Hopkins Medical School open. It was a huge success. By the time of the flu epidemic of 1918, with brilliant work done by the Hopkins in Baltimore, the Rockefeller Institute for Medical Research in New York, and some universities, America had caught up with Europe. A handful of American leaders emerged and worked to transform the life sciences and medicine.

Among scientists, there was a huge race to find the pathogen that caused influenza. Cries for help from the public put enormous pressure on them. Laboratories worked feverishly to develop a vaccine. The pressure was so high that several laboratories offered vaccines to the public only on the wishful hope that they would work. There was no time for trials to prove their efficacy, so there was no guarantee. A government agency like the Food and Drug Administration to step in and exert some control was years in the future. In fact, despite the urgency, it would be more than ten years, in 1928, that the influenza virus would be identified in papers published by Richard Shop.

Since doctors did not have any approved scientific treatment, in desperation, many tried their cures in an attempt to save lives. Results didn't bear them out, and some of these bordered on the absurd. The percentage of deaths from these random experiments was high, but, even so, many claimed success. A few even resorted to the long-discredited remedy of bleeding. The Journal of the American Medical Association published therapies that doctors tried, anything that seemed to make sense, without endorsing any of them.

Cautious by nature, Nixon did not experiment, nor was he tempted to try any of the suggested therapies. Nixon knew that the disease had to run its course, and if you got up from your sickbed too soon, it would come back to bite you. He observed that the patients who listened to him and stayed in bed, survived, and the ones who refused and kept on going developed complications or died. Men would feel better and plunge into work after a week or two and then collapse and die without warning. There was a thin line between life and death. Body aches were so intense that people could hardly move. Yet, to force patients to take his advice and stay in bed, he decided to withhold aspirin and deny them temporary relief as a life-saving measure.

The scientific explanation for sudden deaths came years. With their immune systems compromised, secondary bacterial infections invaded the patients' lungs, and they died from pneumonia. It is generally agreed among scientists and epidemiologists that the majority of influenza deaths in the pandemic came from bacterial pneumonia.

Late in the epidemic, a vaccine became available named after Camp Sherman, a military camp in Ohio whose morbidity rate had been the highest in the country. Nixon was fortunate to be able to obtain a supply of the Sherman vaccine, as it was called so that he could inoculate people, although he didn't hold out much hope for it. As he expected, the vaccine proved to be ineffective and was just a panacea. Although it didn't help his patients, it benefited him immensely. People in the patch were reassured and felt protected, and the unwarranted criticism he was getting stopped.

In late September, Nixon received word that his brother, Bill, a corporal in the 319th infantry, had been killed in France on September 26, 1918. On that day, the Meuse-Argonne offensive was launched by the French and American troops for a final assault on the Hindenburg line. This was the most massive United States offensive of a war that had raged for four years. Bill was killed by a direct hit from a shell, and his death came just a little over a month before the armistice, November 11, 1918.

He lost his life in this last significant battle of the war, only four months after he left the States, and three days before his 25th birthday.

This news of Bill's death was a crushing blow. It came when Nixon was exhausted, engulfed each day in sickness, and overwhelmed with the sorrow of others. Close in age, he and Bill had shared a happy childhood. Nixon wanted to go home. He wanted to be with his grieving parents, not only for their sake but for his own. He needed the comfort of the family. But he had to put aside his grief. He could not leave Revere in distress without another doctor to take his place.

CHAPTER 16

Other Natural Immune Helpers

Ginger

Everyone knows that ginger is particularly suitable for sore throats and nausea, but where's the evidence, and why is this true? It's an excellent antioxidant and anti-inflammatory. It does help suppress bacterial infections in the throat and tonsils, supports healthy immunity, and is coming to the fore due to its anti-cancer effects. It's also good for cardiovascular health. There's not much published on it showing antiviral results. However, a study tested its effects, compared with garlic, on chick embryo cells infected with 'bird flu' and found ginger. Garlic had an evident antiviral activity, which increased with higher doses.

I tend to think of ginger more for soothing sore throats than as an antiviral agent. However, this study shows the basis for an antiviral effect. The issue is how to get a high 'dose.' While chopping up bits of ginger and letting it soak does give you some ginger, how do you squeeze the 'juice' out of the ginger? Also, inevitably when a cold or flu strikes, I find I've run out. So here's a hot tip. Find someone with a juicer or get one yourself. Buy a large amount of ginger and make a cup of pure ginger juice. Pour this into an ice cube tray and freeze it. Then, when you get a cold, you can pop out two, pour on boiling water, a squeeze of lemon, and some honey or agave and drink this. You can also add vitamin C powder as vitamin C is not destroyed by hot water. Alternatively, put lots of finely chopped ginger into a thermos and let it steep for 15 minutes.

Garlic

Garlic is antiviral, anti-fungal, and antibacterial. Rich in sulfur-containing amino acids, it also acts as an antioxidant. It is undoubtedly a critical ally in fighting infections, and garlic-eaters have a lower incidence of cancer. I like to eat a clove a day, in food, but increase this when fighting infections.

It's aged garlic taken in substantial amounts. When garlic is aged over 20 months in aqueous ethanol, it concentrates antioxidants and becomes more potent.

In a 90 day study in which 120 healthy volunteers were given 2.6g of aged garlic (three 1g tablets of aged garlic), not only did they produce more T-cells and N.K. cells, which functioned better, but also fared better when they had a cold or flu, compared to placebo. Much like vitamin C, they didn't get fewer colds or flu.

Another placebo-controlled trial, but not on colds, showed that 3.6g of aged garlic (four tablets) reduced inflammation and promoted more and healthier immune cells.

I buy old garlic tablets (1,000mg per pill – see Resources for suppliers) and take ten or even 20 at a time or throughout the day. That's a lot more than considered in this study because I find it rapidly clears an infection. I know of no study testing this effect, but plenty of people who swear by it. It's a non-toxic option.

Getting Enough Sleep, Keep Fit, Reduce Stress and Stay Warm

The first is sleep. It has a direct effect on your immunity, and too little increases inflammation and depresses immunity, thus increasing your chance of picking up an infection. Shift workers, for example, get more colds. Also, when you are sick, your body knows that you need more sleep, which helps support a healthy immune response. In most health-related studies, the most youthful people sleep between seven and eight hours a night, relatively uninterrupted. You may need more when you're fighting an infection. But don't get less. If you do get less than six hours of sleep a night, or have very disturbed sleep, this will have a knock-on effect on your immunity.

Keeping fit is similar to sleep. Too much depletes immunity. An example is a marathon running. Marathon runners are often used to test the effects of potential cold remedies since it is widespread to get a cold after a marathon. But no exercise depletes immunity, too. While there's no good evidence, specifically on chills, vital energy-generating activity such as yoga has been shown to have positive effects on immunity. So, keep yourself fit. A good guideline is to do three 30 minutes' cardio' exercise sessions a week, getting your heart rate up – this could be brisk walking, jogging, swimming, cycling; and three 'resistance' sessions a week which, if focused, can be done in under 8 minutes.

Stress plays a big part in health and, although we are designed to deal with short-term anxiety, chronic ongoing stress depletes immunity and increases the risk of infection.

During infection, it's good to stay warm by, for example, having a hot bath and drinking hot drinks. If you get bunged up doing inhalations by making a basin of hot water with a few drops of Oblas oil and inhaling this with a towel over your head can help. It is steam, as opposed to warm dry air, that helps to clear the mucus out of airways.

In summary, as part of your immune defense strategy:

• Have lots of ginger in drinks and soups, garlic and shake in food as well as red onions, broccoli, and blueberries

• Make sure you get enough sleep, stay warm, keep fit and control your stress levels.

• Consider having a high dose of aged garlic, 10g, or more if you're finding it hard to shift an infection.

• Experiment with Echinacea as an add-on remedy but don't rely on this only.

• Eat shiitake mushrooms frequently. It is available in dried form from Chinese supermarkets as well as online and is an excellent addition to soups, stews, and stir-fries.

• Take a medicinal mushroom supplement if you are prone to infections.

CHAPTER 17 Why We Were Extremely Close To A SARS Pandemic and How It Was Prevented

Moving into more recent history, we have also dealt with a potential pandemic in this century, but we managed to prevent it. It was the SARS (sudden acute respiratory syndrome) infection that spread starting in November 2002 and eventually killed 774 people and infected 8,000.

A Reminder of What Happened

The first cases appeared in November 2002 in Guangdong Province in China. In February 2003, a victim unknowingly brought the virus to Hong Kong, where he infected international guests. By early March, there were cases in Hong Kong, Toronto, Singapore, and Vietnam. Two days after, it announced travel alerts.

Researchers acted fast, and by March 17, there were 11 labs across nine countries working on it, coordinated by the WHO. CDC researchers and those in Hong Kong isolated the new virus that was present in SARS patients. By May 4th, scientists knew how long the infection could last on surfaces and in waste. By the end of the month, Guangdong Province and Hong Kong were both cleared as safe for travel.

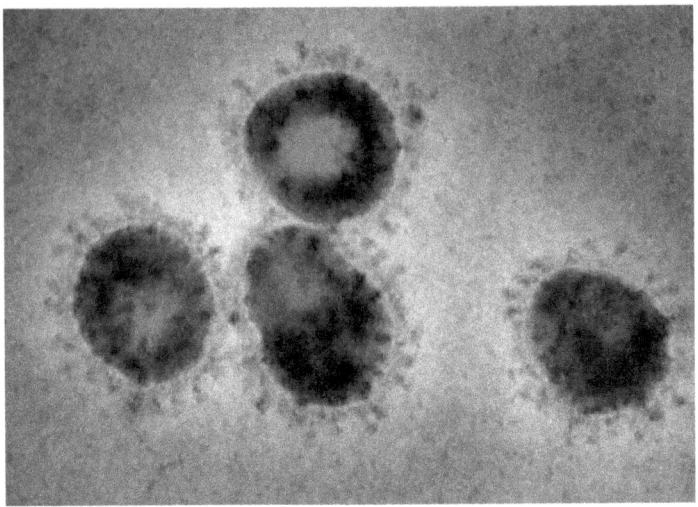

Laboratories Working Together Prevented the Pandemic

The fact that government leaders and scientists from around the world worked together is what allowed us to prevent the SARS outbreak from turning into an epidemic. The 11 laboratories across nine countries worked together towards a shared problem, and the teams allowed this common goal to overcome rivalries, both at the individual and national level. Instead, the focus was on collaboration with health care workers, scientists, and government officials, all playing a pivotal role.

China's Initial Reaction Did Cause Issues

Even with the successful prevention of the SARS pandemic, there were more infections and deaths than there could have been. At first, China refused to share vital data with others. It means that when the first international cases occurred, the local governments and health care workers were unprepared.

China's lack of information sharing also extended to delivering accurate reports. It was not until April 20th that Chinese authorities announced there were more cases than they had reported and that the officials who published the misleading statements were no longer in office.

Correcting this misinformation problem was able to help get prevention back on track.

Clear Communication Helped Prevent a Pandemic

In addition to the collaboration, clear communication between policymakers, scientists, and the public helped limit the spread of SARS and get it under control. The CDC was clear with United States citizens about its knowledge, and people took advantage of the information available to them.

The extent to which the CDC ensured communication remained open. The SARS website for the CDC had more than 17 million hits within the outbreak. During the time, it also had 12 press releases, 12 live news conferences, and briefings, and answered 35,000 phone calls from the general public and 10,000 from the media. It also set up 30 conference calls with health care providers and a hotline for doctors that received more than 2,000 calls.

This general information ensured that doctors and public officials who came across SARS knew what to expect, including in terms of symptoms and treatment.

CHAPTER 18

Epidemiology

Epidemiology is the branch of medicine concerned with researching factors related to the distribution of disease in human populations. Essential components of epidemiological research include studying the cause, incidence, prevalence, behavior, and transmission of disease affecting groups of people. Epidemiology is most often associated with public health since it is primarily concerned with disease outbreaks in human populations, in contrast to disease manifestation in individuals. Depending on research needs, the community studied can be of any size and composition as extended members of the group share specific characteristics relevant to the researcher. For instance, study populations can be based on geography, where people as large as individual nations or entire continents are examined. Conversely, communities may be as small a remote village or a single worksite where all individuals are exposed to identical environmental toxins, such as airborne coal dust inhaled by workers at a local coal mine. While geography is often an essential consideration in epidemiological research, groups can also be studied based on numerous factors unrelated to a physical location, such as age, gender, race or nationality, diet, and so on.

Since epidemiology and pathology both study disease, people often find it difficult to distinguish between the two scientific disciplines. Easy, although the vastly simplified way to differentiate is that epidemiology is the study of disease in groups of people. In contrast, pathology studies illness in a person or organism.

Morbidity and Disease

Two of the most basic and essential concepts in Epidemiology are incidence and prevalence. Incidence and prevalence are both measures of morbidity. Quite merely, morbidity is the extent of illness, injury, or disability in a defined population. In epidemiology, incidence and prevalence are substantial in that both statistics attempt to measure risk, where risk is the likelihood that an individual within a society will contract a disease. While both incidence and prevalence attempt to estimate the occurrence of a health condition during a specified period, many people confuse incidence and prevalence and use them interchangeably falsely assuming that one is simply a synonym for the other. However, when researching Avian Influenza, it is crucial to remember that each term has a distinct meaning.

The term incidence refers to the number of new cases of a health condition in a given time. In other words, the extent most closely resembles the number of new diagnoses. Conversely, prevalence means the number of persons currently suffering from a health condition. In this regard, a person diagnosed with a chronic health condition (where chronic describes an illness persisting over a long time) will be included in incidence statistics in only one year, that being the year they were

101

diagnosed. Still, this same individual will be involved in prevalence reports each year they suffer this health condition. Take one step further, a newly diagnosed patient will be counted in both incidence and prevalence statistics during the patient's first year of a health condition but in subsequent years will only be included in prevalence statistics. The important takeaway, therefore, is that for any given timeframe, the prevalence of a health condition will always be equal or higher than the incidence of the same situation. Most of the time, frequency, and prevalence statistics are reported on an annual basis, though for health conditions like Influenza, seasonal or monthly morbidity may be more critical.

Because these two concepts have distinct meanings, they are most revealing taken together, and often the two numbers can vary dramatically from one another. For short-lived health conditions like Influenza, incidence can be very high during years with large outbreaks as large populations may suffer from a vaccine-resistant Influenza strain. Still, the overall prevalence may be quite low in subsequent years. On the other hand, for some chronic illnesses, the incidence rate may be flat when compared to the prevalence rate. An example is when public health researchers introduce new preventative treatment strategies for a particular health condition. Currently, enormous resources are being used to prevent Type II Diabetes. However, if preventative efforts are successful, we can expect the number of new diagnoses in the first "successful" year to decline dramatically. Therefore, in that year, the incidence of the disease will significantly decrease, but those already afflicted with the condition may still keep the prevalence statistics high.

If, for example, you notice that incidence and prevalence rates are both high for nine (9) consecutive years, but the incidence rate drops dramatically in the tenth year you may rightly hypothesize that a new preventative treatment was introduced in the tenth year, therefore, leading you to research your assumption further.

It is also important to remember that incidence and prevalence statistics do not attempt to measure the entire population. Instead, these statistics generally measure people at risk. To illustrate, incidence and prevalence measures of Cervical Cancer only include women. Likewise, Testicular Cancer is only calculated for men. While this is important to remember, the research you will discover will report the population the estimate is intended to reflect.

Mathematically, with "/" meaning "divided by" the calculations for incidence and prevalence can be expressed as follows:

Incidence Rate = Number of New Cases within a given time / Number of People at Risk of Getting the Disease

Prevalence Rate = Total Number of Cases at a Single Point in Time / Number of People at Risk of Getting the Disease

Multiply the result by 100 or 1000 to get the number of a person to get the number of cases per 100 or 1000, respectively.

Finally, remember that incidence and prevalence statistics are only estimates and not an entirely exact reflection of the population being measured. For example, for some health disorders, the incidence rate can be higher than the actual number of people affected by a health condition. A typical example is incidence reports for the common cold. Many individuals may get a common cold two or more times in a given year and, therefore, will be counted multiple times in incidence statistics even though they are only one person. Likewise, some prevalence measures estimating the occurrence of a particular cancer type, for instance, may include persons in remission where other prevalence estimates do not.

Sources of Morbidity Statistics

Morbidity statistics are aggregated and collected by many organizations. Some organizations that collect this data include:

1.   Hospitals and clinics

2.   Disease and cancer registries

3.   Communicable disease reporting surveillance public health agencies

4.   Vital statistics

5.   Surveys

6.   Health and life insurance plans

CHAPTER 19

Yogic Role in Managing Pandemic Swine Flu or Influenza an (H1N1)

A Chairman and Managing Director of a reputed hospital, who were a very hard-working type, wanted to understand how to become an award winner for the services provided by his hospital. He was equally eager to know the procedure to be adopted to serve the clients & community better so that the reputation gained during services could be retained for long. To see the concept behind, he approached a modern management guru. He asked him, Sir, how can I build the personality & professional ability both among the managerial staff so that they can perform their best to serve the community?

The management Guru replied, "There are two important factors in the management scenario, namely efficiency, and effectiveness which show the progressive health of the management. They are related to personality and professional ability of the management staff respectively".

In the field of management, the efficiency of a manager is the procedure defined as a result obtained (output) divided by the measures taken in (input).

In other words, the efficiency is the ratio of maximum output obtained against maximum input given.

Similarly, the effectiveness of the team is distinct by the overall growth obtained divided by the planning and other inputs given by the management people.

He further explained that the efficiency of the system is dependent on the personality of managerial staff in the organization, which, in turn, is reliant on the inner awareness of the management staff. The character of the managing staff is proportional to (i) the purification of their five sheaths (body) (ii) utility of body, mind, intellect, and self (iii) internal awareness in respect of how best the people are free from the inner dialogue to save the energy (iv) how wisely the people have understood four (inner instrument) (v) how best the people utilize the positive attitude.

Similarly, he narrated the effectiveness of the system, which depends on professional ability and overall outer awareness of the people engaged in a management scenario. For instance, how good people are in professional skills, disciplined in their behavior, and trained in a particular field.

To the effectiveness of the system, there is a dire need for growth in outer awareness among the managerial staff. The management people are required to be right in an inter-personal relationship while dealing with the people, to have total quality management concepts in respect of items, to have the teamwork approach using motivational theories at a different scenario, and to have the growth of multi-tasking ability to deal with the situations.

Management guru further briefed that people comprise three characteristics for growing their personality and professional ability. They are

(i) Attitude involving feeling, approach and belief system at head level

(ii) Potentiality consisting of aspiration, resources & source of becoming at heart level and (iii) Aptitude utilizing capability, ability, and bent upon nature to explore the punch at hands level.

When the managers are going to combine attitude with evolve potential (usually potential remains dormant), then they grow the best possible personality. Likewise, when they make a union of aptitude with expanded potential, they perform well & their professional ability is well developed. If the people combine the aspects of three elements-- Head, Heart & Hands together, then they have the best professional capacity with a happy personality.

Typically, the potentiality remains hidden at the inner nature of an individual, which can be brought out with the help of Yogic awareness. In a nutshell, the professional growth & the best possible performance can be enhanced with the help of tuning the attitude along with hidden potential and also regulating the aptitude amid evolved potential. The concept of blending the attitude & ability, along with potentiality, is explained with the help of a diagram.

The attitude of the people works like a mirror where one can see one's reflection related to inner dialogue, whereas aptitude facilitates like spectacle so that the vision of external awareness can be grown. Attitude helps to develop emotional consciousness, and in turn, personality is developed.

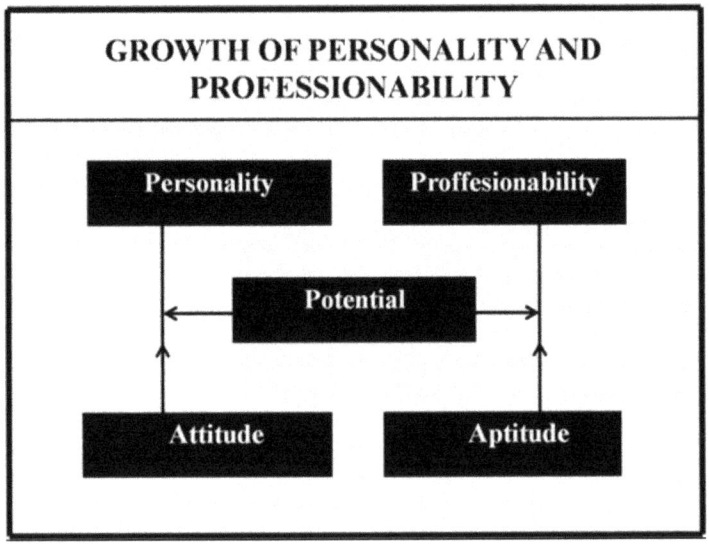

The diagram explains the concept of blending attitude, potential ability, and aptitude to retain the best possible personality with excellent performance.

Attitude and Aptitude will lead towards a positive approach whenever there is a growth in Yogic awareness. In the case of a negative approach, there is a chance that Yogic knowledge lags. Typically, the positive approach may not guarantee success; however, it provides an easy way to tackle the problems and situations. However, the negative attitude ensures failure.

World Health Organization (WHO) is committed to providing better management to maintain the normal health of the people, even in the case of pandemic Influenza (H1N1). For that, they have prepared a solid table "WHO pandemic phase descriptions and main actions by phase" to combat the pandemic effect. It needs no deficiency in the services likely to be rendered by WHO management. It is possible when the faculties like the head, heart, and hands of each management staff function together in a positive direction. It is feasible when each one would have developed the Yogic awareness in oneself.

That is why WHO needs the development of Yogic awareness along with modern scientific development to combat crisis management like the post-pandemic period and post-peak period of Influenza (H1N1), including its severity.

CHAPTER 20

Management Planned by WHO

T he table "WHO pandemic phase descriptions and main actions by phase" has been prepared by W.H.O for the welfare of people. The table emphasizes on

(i) Planning and coordination (ii) situation monitoring and assessment (iii) communication (iv) reducing the spread of disease and (v) continuity of health care provision points for the effective management of Influenza A (H1N1).

W.H.O is facing two challenges like the post-pandemic period and the post-peak period. It has planned to obtain and distribute the vaccine as a preventive measure, so that spread of pandemic is checked or minimized. At the same time, WHO has also intended to curb the severity of Influenza A(H1N1) by adopting the distribution of proper medicine as curative measures. The therapeutic action is essential when the virus is already spread and has taken the shelter to sustain at host cells of the body.

W.H.O has meticulously planned for the best possible leadership to coordinate the multi-spectral resources to mitigate the social and economic impact. Besides, active monitoring, continuous updating of the information required for curbing the risk, implementation of the pharmaceutical measure, and contingency plan for the health system at all levels have also been included.

It has taken the best possible preventive measures to obtain high efficiency by minimizing and slowing down the spread of viruses. Likewise, the medical means given for the therapeutic approach is also effective until the infection is not changing its structure containing H1 and N1 subtypes.

The WHO plan will be quite effective only for the Influenza A(H1N1) until it retains its sub-types. Any change in sub-types (structure of virus) will create a question mark for the effective use of the medicines developed in context with Influenza A(H1N1).

The risk, severity & complexity of Influenza A(H1N1) can be appropriately handled, provided the hidden potentiality of the employees of working organization is brought out as service mission.

Views about pandemic

Whenever three conditions are met, the resultant effect is pandemic. The terms are namely (i) infectious virus (ii) spreading because of cross-contamination and (iii) when a virus can sustain in the human system for a longer time. Until condition number (i) & (ii) are met, and condition (iii) does not exist, the scenario will not be pandemic.

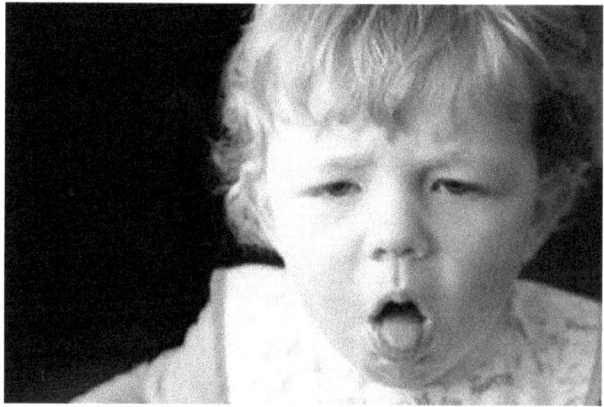

The spread of Influenza A(H1N1) can become pandemic through air travel when the infectious virus comes out because of coughing, sneezing & spiting. It becomes the reason for spreading in the human environment due to cross-contamination, and the same can sustain if the virus remains strong.

World Health Organization's survey shows that the pandemic virus can cause the death rate quite high in a profoundly affected community, especially in developing countries. The experience shows that a developed country like the USA had a low mortality rate in the past because of stringent medical measures taken there.

However, during a pandemic, all countries are likely to experience emergency conditions, and they need inter-country assistance. It has also been observed in the past whenever there was a natural disaster.

 The effect of a pandemic can be curtailed more effectively once the alternate methodology is available other than the medication and hospitalization. Though, World Health Organization and member countries are alert and aware of the pandemic effect; they need an alternate logistic approach as a supplementary approach so that the difficulty related to the development of vaccines and shortage of medicines can be overcome.

It is difficult to prevent the pandemic because of its severity having a widespread effect in nature and natural sustainability in the human system. It is tough to remove the virus from the environment as it finds its shelter in the shadow area on a sunny day without losing its life and comes out when it detects a conducive environment. The effect of the existing virus from the atmosphere, Jain monks, had suggested not taking food in the night so that the chances of the infection to go inside the human body are restricted.

Pregnant women are vulnerable, like everyone, and they should take all the necessary precautions.

CHAPTER 21

Preventing Future Outbreaks Relevant To Ebola

It is particularly relevant for Ebola endemic countries in the great lakes region and tropical rain forest belt of sub-Saharan Africa.

What is of particular concern in these areas is the relatively frequent Ebola outbreaks that imply high-level human-animal contact, especially that most of these animals tend to be wild.

This increased human-animal contact may be attributed to the proximity of local communities to rainforests as well as the degradation of the natural habitats of wild animals and fruit bats. This fact necessitates the need for continuing efforts to reduce the risk of such human-wild animal or human-bat contact to minimize the risk of new outbreaks.

One of the most important strategies is to convince local communities to desist from hunting wild animals such as monkeys, chimpanzees, and bats for food. I adhered to this can potentially reduce contact with them.

It is believed that halting the hunting and consumption of wild animals and bats have the potential to reduce the risk such behavior poses concerning disease transmission significantly.

While enormous efforts have been expended towards discouraging consumption of "bush meat," there have been counter voices that prefer more focus on their culinary practices.

In summary, all these efforts are geared towards ensuring that human-bat and human-wild animal contact is minimized. This strategy is emphasized because Ebola outbreaks usually occur when direct or indirect contact is made with infected bats or wild animals, regardless of whether they are dead or alive!

As has been shown in outbreaks in the DRC, Sudan, Uganda, and West Africa, local populations need to be continuously educated about the Ebola virus and the disease, with specific emphasis on how individuals and communities can protect themselves and others from the deadly Ebola virus disease!

Infection Control and Prevention

Another important issue that surrounds Ebola outbreaks is how to keep infections at bay once there is an outbreak. While some of the problems may appear inhumane, the highly infectious nature of the disease requires that health workers have to exhibit a high level of care while caring for the patients. To limit the spread of infection, isolation of patients is paramount during outbreaks.

Several strategies exist to help minimize the spread of an ongoing epidemic within hospitals and in affected communities.

In hospitals, patients have to be cared for under strict barrier nursing. It involves avoiding direct contact with the body and body fluids of the patient, including aerosols, through the use of specially designed *"Ebola body armor,"* which allows caregivers to seal themselves off effectively-right from head to toe.

Whenever possible, hospitalized patients should be kept under specially designed High-Efficiency Particulate (HEPA) respirators. This confinement protects clinical staff against aerosols coming from patients' coughs and sneezes.

These unique air purifiers remove airborne particles, thus preventing possible spread of viruses through aerosols produced by Ebola patients.

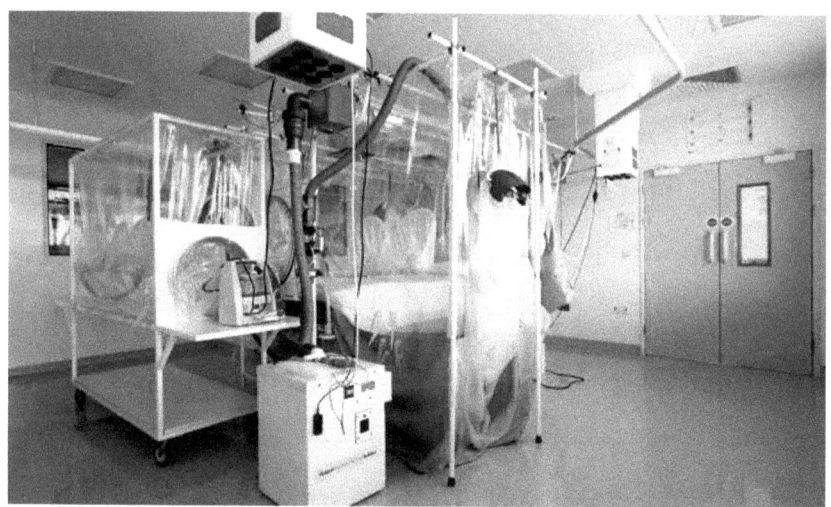

A high-grade infectious disease isolation unit via Royal Free Hospital, London

In addition to barrier nursing techniques and air purifiers, health workers are also expected to limit injections. Furthermore, caregivers are required to handle blood, secretions, catheters, and suction devices, and non-disposable equipment with great care.

118

These infection control techniques are aimed at minimizing infection transmission possibilities to the clinical health workers themselves as well as other non-health workers in the hospital.

Besides careful clinical management of patients, another vital strategy of Ebola care is excellent laboratory services. For best results, the World Health Organization recommends these labs should be established at the start of an epidemic to enable health teams to identify quickly, quarantine, and manage Ebola patients.

As an infection prevention strategy, lab workers are also expected to exercise great care while handling blood and body fluid samples that are being used for diagnosis and monitoring the disease progress.

Since lab workers are at risk, samples are only handled by trained staff and processed in specially equipped laboratories, termed BSL-4 laboratories where the risk for infection is reduced.

Apart from the careful management of Ebola patients in hospitals, risk reduction is a critical component of infection prevention and control in community settings. A strategy that has been used with a measure of success in recent times is community engagement.

The primary purpose of engaging communities is to raise awareness of risk factors that ease infection spread. Besides, it also helps in promoting the measures that individuals within the community can take to reduce human-to-human transmission.

Usually, awareness creation and social mobilization are done by educating members of the community about the disease, dispelling

119

rumors, and providing information on how every member of the affected population can stay free from Ebola.

Awareness creation also involves educating the masses about the actions of teams. Amid epidemics in East, Central, and West Africa, increasing community awareness has been done through the house to house talks, radios, television, and by involving local cultural and religious leaders because of their influence.

Ebola outreach community mobilization ©WHO/MA Heine

As communities are mobilized against ongoing outbreaks, surveillance and contact tracing teams also work alongside community educators. Their main task is usually to help identify and compile the lists of people, whether dead or alive, who may have been in contact with infected persons. This practice of *"contact tracing"* helps to identify potential patients fast.

Apart from *contact tracing*, hospital-based medical workers surveillance teams alongside also monitor the wellbeing of contacts for at least 21 days. Whenever they develop Ebola-like symptoms, then they are promptly referred for hospitalization. Another primary infection prevention strategy that straddles across the hospital and the community is the establishment of burial teams. This team, which comprises trained personnel, conducts a safe burial of deceased Ebola victims in designated areas.

Burial of Ebola victims in Uganda

Yet another strategy is training burial team members to desist from washing and embalming the body of deceased patients. And when burying the dead, teams have to wear personal protective equipment. The picture depicts the work and technique of the trained burial teams, which are essential for controlling and eliminating an ongoing Ebola epidemic.

CHAPTER 22

How to Survive a Pandemic without Killing Nerve Cells: Psychological Tips

The coronavirus pandemic continues in the world: a terrible infection became a fatal challenge for society, took thousands of lives, and "locked" people in homes across the globe. For two weeks, Dave also lives and works in quarantine. The forced limitation of opportunities, the continuous flow of information, and the uncertainty of the future easily disorient everyone. And in such conditions, it is essential not to lose both physical and psychological health.

What internal dangers can lie in wait for each of us, and why are they no less severe than the disease caused by viruses? What will help to deal with your feelings during a pandemic and forced isolation? How not to quarrel with relatives and friends during the quarantine period? What to do to avoid depression? Psychologist Michelle answers these and other questions.

Together with her colleagues in a pandemic, she became the operator of the "hotline" of psychological assistance for those who are oppressed by the current situation.

Michelle, first of all, let me thank you for helping others to cope with the difficult times. It is essential. Tell me how many people have already turned to the "hotline"? How can you generally evaluate the psychological state of people in a given period?

I can say that there are predominantly conscious citizens who adhere to quarantine conditions and are at home. If when they go outside, but with protective equipment. Yes, some take the situation not very seriously and let the children go for a walk or go company themselves. They were not so responsive to quarantine, and, perhaps, simply do not orient themselves sufficiently in the situation. As for panic or tension in society, they are more felt on the Internet than in life. Everyone is worried that they cannot go to work, and especially those with a private business. And the material side of citizens is more concerned than psychological.

We can observe a very different attitude towards the pandemic. Many initially denied the problem and only now realized its seriousness. Some people came to terms with quarantine, and some even began to rejoice that nature was resting from people, and in general, there could be positive changes in the world.

Yes, we can say that the public mood now corresponds to this particular scheme. That is, at first, it seems to us that this is some kind of joke, that this is happening somewhere very far away and not with us. Then people begin to realize that it is a few steps away from them, and that is reality. Many begin to show fear, panic, and disorientation in their own lives. It became possible to find positive things in quarantine: you can also communicate with your loved ones and do those things for which there was not enough time before. It is the stage of acceptance of the situation and adaptation. Now we are more responsive to our actions, we understand the consequences of our actions and try to cope with it.

During the spread of the coronavirus, people with an increased sense of empathy were confronted with a feeling of powerlessness in front of the world, because they could not influence what had happened. How common is this?

Psychologists often face the fact that people give up because they cannot influence the general situation. We try to draw their attention to the fact that if everyone does what depends on him, we can thus contribute to the big picture and fight the pandemic. When everyone takes even small steps towards the struggle, this will be our control over the situation. When we talk, think, do, then we will help the state, our settlement, and all of humanity.

You are talking about panic, fear for life, and health. Is this the most comfortable way or the most logical? What to do with these moods?

This crisis in many people exacerbates sensitivity to stressful processes. It is better, of course, if possible, to consult a specialist. Unfortunately, we still have not fully developed a culture of psychological literacy. If this is not possible, we recommend that you deal more with your internal state in the here and now situation. To ask myself: "How can I help myself specifically when I cannot influence the situation as a whole?" When it's hard to accept a situation, it's best to start with yourself.

What about panic in social networks? Around a lot of people who disagree with each other. And it's challenging for people to accept that many do not think like you. How to stop wasting time and nerves in disputes?

People spend a lot of energy on proving something to someone. I, as a specialist, understand that inclusion in some disputes and evidence - this primarily means that there are a lot of fears inside a person. And he thus tries to either confirm them or refute them. It is at a symbolic level the transfer of terror into some other activity. It seems to people that when they prove that the coronavirus is dangerous, and everyone will be afraid, it will appear to be easier for them. The dissemination of various unconfirmed information, which provokes panic and fear, suggests that people do not have critical thinking and cannot recognize truthful information. I would recommend to be critical of any information and not to engage in disputes, evidence-based conversations and, if possible, check the information before, then her to pass her on and trust her. It is also essential to track your reactions and ask yourself, "When I share with her, what do I want to get? To make people perk up? Or do I want everyone to be afraid together with me, and it will feel better for me?"

To some extent, someone argues on social networks and out of idleness. Today, a lot of people ended up at home. What can you advise regarding the organization of the day and life at home so that isolation does not lead to depression?

First: if you live with your loved ones in the same house or apartment, then, first of all, communicate more with these people. Take time for your children, older people. Focus on them and not lock yourself.

Second: you can do creativity. Those who have experience in keeping a diary can record and record thoughts, actions. It is an emotional discharge. You can engage in various creative activities, directly probing what you want to do, what is best given. It can be drawing and singing and playing musical instruments and general events with loved ones.

Third: nature is also a reliable resource for us. Those who have plants, animals at home can do them. Firstly, it takes a lot of time, and secondly, it is beneficial. If you have a private house, you can go outside, breathe air, enjoy what we now have the opportunity to contemplate. Let in some temporary isolation, however, see the positive side in silence, in the absence of the usual troubles. If a person is religious, he can devote time to communicate with God, chat with like-minded people in various ways.

And the fourth: quarantine is, first of all, the time that we can devote to our children. They are at home during the absence of the educational process. And now there is a maximum of opportunities to establish communication with children, to strengthen relationships.

Just before quarantine, there was less opportunity to communicate with relatives and children. Now that the distance has been reduced, how can one not quarrel with them and better smooth out conflict situations?

I agree, there is a downside here. We cannot rest from loved ones. All family members are long in one limited space, and there is a risk of conflict. I would advise first of all to ask myself questions: "What do I feel?" and "What do others feel?", "What is important to me? and "What is important to another person?" When we talk about our feelings, it is more comfortable. When we think about the opinions of others, it helps us understand the motives and needs of loved ones. And talk. Do not accumulate feelings, emotions, and thoughts in yourself, but speak them. And give yourself the opportunity for e-tactics to be alone with themselves. Give others a break from you. It is not necessary to be in different rooms, and you can distinguish between activities, the distribution of responsibilities.

Isolation is the creation of a situation of artificial stress. To overcome it, you first need to think: "Why is something causing me stress?" "How can I help myself?" "How can I help another person?". And then, if people still enter into dialogue, they will be able to find some kind of mutual understanding of their needs, motives, and desires, and reach some sort of compromise.

What can you advise to increase concentration at work at home?

Understanding when you do chores at home, it is best to write a plan of the day in the morning after waking up. The idea of the week is, of course, ideal, but at least the outline of tasks for "today," a kind of schedule. It should indicate what you should, say, do before lunch, after work, and so on. Today there is a maximum of opportunities to use Internet resources to communicate with colleagues, clients, and other people on work issues remotely. And by the way, you can devote a lot of time to your self-development, through the same online courses, and online resources. It is best to first set yourself at least for a day, some clear working goal, and make a second list, for example, for household chores. When a person has a specific plan, it's easier for him to focus on his tasks and fulfill that plan,

Jamming and drinking stress. What to do to prevent this from becoming a habit?

"Jamming" and "drinking" stress has now become especially relevant because it is also a way to deal with stress. Everyone, based on their experience, today can quickly begin to abuse some of their habits to help themselves deal with the crisis. It's better to find other ways and stick to a healthy lifestyle. Limit yourself to food directly is not worth it, but when choosing products, it is better to stick to those that do not cause excitement. For example, it is better not to include very salty foods or dishes with too bright pronounced taste properties in the diet. It is worth paying more attention to healthy sleep, healthy eating, and physical activity. Focus on facts so as not to aggravate your condition and understand that the crisis will someday end.

CHAPTER 23

Bad Habits That Can Make Us Sick

W e all have bad habits that can make us sick and challenge our immune system. If you or your family members are often ill, it is time to look at your lifestyle. Some of these habits are very addicting, and if a person cannot get out to purchase such things as cigarettes, alcohol, or recreational drugs, withdrawals can take over. Why not start today, to alleviate yourself from these habits. It is something to think about before disaster strikes. A step at a time in the right direction will help you build up your immune system and be good for your mental health. We have found that it takes 21 days to break a habit. Those mentioned above are other bad habits that we need to replace with good habits to stay healthy and to help keep others healthy.

Do Not Go Out Sick

It is not always easy to stay at home when you are ill. Life goes on. The problem is when you are sick with a cold, flu, or another contagious disease, you are spreading it to others.

We all need our paycheck and sad to say if we stay home, we could lose our jobs. Many businesses require a doctor's note to receive paid sick days. Some people do not have insurance, and it is a financial hardship to go to the doctor. No matter what, fess up. Do not go to work with a cold feigning "allergies." Let others know so they can take precautions. Wear a mask. Stay away from co-workers. Do not make stops and run errands on the way to and from work. If you are sick, skip church, meetings, and social gatherings. Do not cook food and bring it to a potluck. Please do everything you can not to spread your germs to others.

Sick Children

It can be another "sore" spot. Children get sick a lot, and Moms and Dads must work. That means if your child is sick, as long as they can walk and are not running a high fever, they usually end up in school or daycare. Once again, honesty is the best policy. If possible, keep your sick child home. All parents who work should have a backup babysitter to care for sick children. Yes, it is an inconvenience, and it can cost money. Think about it. Do you want your child exposed to sickness at school or daycare? Surely not. So please keep that in mind when sending a child out. Also, skip birthday parties and other social activities until your child is no longer contagious.

Poor Diet

As we mentioned above, the immune system needs a clean diet. We suggest you avoid sugar. Ridding sugar from your diet is a significant step to good health. You do not have to quit all at once. Keep a log for one week, writing down each time you eat processed sugar. You do not need to write down how many teaspoons or grams, just how many times you ate sugar. If you eat a candy bar, that counts as one. Ate a piece of cake? That counts as another one. At the end of the week, count how many you had. If you are a big sugar eater, you might want to drop 5-10 sugar eating instances. If your count for the week is 20 or less, you might want to lose 1-3. Keep keeping track until you have quit.

A healthy diet

The following are just a few ideas toward a healthy diet.

- Choose whole foods instead of processed.

- Do not drink sugary drinks, sodas, or caffeine drinks.

- Keep healthy food readily available.

- Eat whole grains and nuts

- Eat on smaller plates to reduce portion size

- Avoid red meat and pork

- Use organic ingredients if possible

- Avoid GMO

- Stay away from fast foods

- Plan your meals ahead of time

- Stay hydrated

There is plenty of information on the internet and at the library to help a person eat a healthy diet. Get rid of the chips, cookies, and sodas in the house, so you are not tempted to eat them. Take one step at a time. Do not overwhelm yourself (Yoder, 2017).

CHAPTER 24

Healthy Living in a Pandemic

PROTEIN

Most of your proteins are going to come from meats, but there are some plant options as well. Proteins are going to need to be either kept cold or frozen so that they don't go wrong. They are not going to be NON-PERISHABLE. That's okay, and we can work around that because they are essential. My suggestion is that you buy enough for around two weeks and maybe more. Keep what is going to be readily used in the fridge and freeze the rest. My parents have a deep freezer full of meat options.

FRUIT

The fruit is going to be super valuable! The reason that they are packed with full micronutrients is going to help keep you healthy. We are currently avoiding sickness, but who knows what else may come our way. We can at least do the best to build up our immune system to fight off anything that could harm us. Vitamin C is one of the essential vitamins that we are going to be after, but the fruit is also suitable for our gut. The fruit is full of fiber that works to feed our gut bacteria. Yes, we have little bugs that reside in our stomachs. They work to keep us healthy, and they, in return, get to feed off of the food in our bellies.

When we aren't correctly eating the right fibers, they don't get to eat . When that happens, we create a recipe for disaster. It can come in the form of brain fog, loss of energy, or even a reduction in our immune response. So, we must keep our fruit intake high for situations like this. Now, how should you store your fruit? Most things, such as berries, oranges, or watermelon, should be in the fridge. Others, such as bananas, can stay at room temp to last even longer.

VEGETABLES

Vegetables are in the same boat as fruits. We need them during these tough times. People typically put a priority on high calories foods in today's world. No, you should not be buying Oreos in preparation for a nationwide crisis. Sure, it's food. However, it is devoid of nutritional value, and it's also hyper-palatable. Meaning, you are more likely to overeat of it and pair that with being bored during isolation, and you'll have none left. The point is that those foods do you no good in a time like this.

GRAINS

You see a massive rush to get these from the store when something such as this happens. People panic to get the most shelf-stable food they can. Well, grains can be pretty shelf-stable. It is because they are what is considered a dry good. They don't have moisture, and things that don't have moisture last longer. So, you may have had a bag of jasmine rice in your pantry for MONTHS, and it's still good. At worst, they can become a little stale if left to the air for too long, but that's what containers were made! Grains are high and will last you well over the amount of time

135

that you are going to be cooped up. I recommend keeping rice on hand, keep beans (canned or dry), and even keep some oatmeal. You can follow the ingredients that are grains as well. Anything made from wheat or barley can be used to create pieces of bread or other baked goods. Keep these on hand, and you can even be a little creative.

FATS

Fats are not always thought of as non-perishable and also not very healthy. However, fats are high! They are part of a balanced diet and perform many functions in the body, and is one of the hormones producers. So, we need these to keep things working the way they should.

CHAPTER 25

Choosing a Secondary Retreat

I f things start to go wrong in the area, you're locked down in, and it may become necessary to retreat to a more secluded area. Having a secondary location, you can head out to is always a good idea, but it's more critical for those living in populated areas. If you live in the epicenter of an outbreak and things go downhill fast, you may have to leave the city and should have a backup plan in place.

The best secondary retreats are in isolated areas that are within an hour or two travel time of the area you're located. While a few hours may not seem like it's far enough away, you have to balance this with the reality that you're probably going to have to fight your way through gridlocked traffic with everyone else who's trying to flee the disease. Choose a remote location where you're unlikely to come in contact with anyone else, and it won't matter that you're still too close for comfort to the outbreak area.

End up spending a significant amount of time living at your secondary retreat, so take extra care to examine both the dwelling and the area around the house carefully.

Here are some questions to ask while walking the property:

- Is there room to plant seeds and grow crops?

- What is winter going to be like in this area? Will the retreat be accessible? If it is, will you be able to live in it?

- Are there plenty of trees and firewood?

- Is the wild game available?

- Are there any natural sources of water nearby? Is it potable? Are there fish that can be caught?

- How likely is it that people driving by will see the retreat? Is it on a busy road that will see lots of traffic? Are there any significant highways or thoroughfares nearby?

- How difficult will it be to defend the property from intruders should you be discovered?

- How hard is it going to be to get to the property if all major roads and highways are blocked or jammed?

- How close are you to densely populated areas?

- Could you walk to this location within 72 hours?

I have several locations mapped out that I can escape. The first one is in the hills within a half-hour of my house. I wouldn't head to this location if travel on the highway were still possible, but it's somewhere

I could walk to in half a day if the roads were blocked, and we had to set off on foot. It is my ideal location because it's a cabin that's off the beaten path, and it's unlikely anyone is going to stumble upon it. If they did, the dogs would alert me long before they made it to the door.

I have a third spot picked out even further away in case I'm forced to leave the second spot for some reason. This spot is even more now off the beaten path, and I would have to hike into it, but it's a great choice if I want to get as far away from civilization as possible.

So, how will you know if it's time to head to your secondary retreat? Many things need to be considered. If you're living in a densely populated area and it looks like the rule of law is crumbling, it's time to get out of there. If the food supply chain breaks down and store shelves are empty for more than a couple days, people are going to be desperate for food and will start looking elsewhere. Packs of armed and potentially-infected people will begin searching house-to-house for food. Your home could become a target, and you'll either have to fight off the bandits or sneak out the back door while they're raiding your home. It's better to gather your supplies and get out of the city while the getting's okay because you'll have a giant target on your back if you're trying to leave with supplies in tow after the rule of law has broken down.

Once you've chosen your secondary retreat (and hopefully a couple more places you can escape to), it's time to sit down and map out multiple routes. The essential roads you're going to need to know are some ways you can get out of town and get headed in the right direction.

Hop on Google Maps and look for smaller country roads and backroads you can use to get out of town. Dirt roads will be less-traveled, but they may be inaccessible in the winter unless you have a four-wheel drive, and even then, they may not be safe. Map out as many routes as you can find and then drive the roads to see what they're.

You may find that some of the roads you found on the map are private roads, and they're gated off. These roads may be a good option when you're looking to get out of town because they won't be gridlocked. Don't cut the lock when you're checking out your routes, but keep a pair of bolt cutters in your vehicle that can be used to cut locks in an emergency.

The Bug Out Bag

The chances of Ebola striking so quickly you don't have time to gather supplies and get out of town is slim-to-none, but it's still a good idea to have a bag with a 72-hour amount of gear, food, and other supplies packed and ready to go you need to get out of the house in a hurry. This type of bag is known as a bug out bag in the prepper and survival community. I recommend packing a bag for each family member who's old enough to carry one. I even have a small backpack for my 7-year old. It doesn't have a lot of stuff in it, but every little bit counts.

Here are some of the items you're going to want to have in a bag:

•   Food. Here's where those MREs and freeze-dried foods can be of benefit. They're small and light, and a bunch of them will fit into a bug out bag without taking up too much space.

•   A basic first aid kit.

•   A cell phone.

•   A compass.

•   A small wind-up radio.

•   Matches

•   Flashlights and batteries.

•   Lighters and fuel.

•   Maps of your planned escape routes.

•   Mess kits.

•   Mylar blankets.

•   Personal documents.

•   Sleeping bags.

•   Tampons.

•   Tent.

•   Toilet paper.

•   Utensils.

- Warm clothing in winter and cool clothing in summer.

- Water purification tablets or filters.

- Water.

Don't forget to pack enough medications to last you until you can get to a pharmacy. While a 72-hour supply of the items above is recommended, it's a good idea to have more than a 72-hour amount of prescription medications in your bag, especially if running out of the medicines could be life-threatening. You never know when you'll have to leave town for an extended time, and having extra pills will help ease the worry that you're going to run out of medicine and get sick.

Body Disposal

Whenever possible, let the professionals handle the disposal of human remains. Disposing of a body yourself is illegal in pretty much all jurisdictions, so keep this in mind if you decide to take matters into your own hands.

The critical thing to remember is that the Ebola virus remains in the body for a long time after a victim dies. What this means is anybody fluids you come in contact with can still infect you hours after the patient has succumbed to Ebola.

The CDC recommends that postmortem care personnel wear the following protective gear when handling bodies:

- Face shield.

- Facemask.

- Impervious gown with full sleeves.

- Shoe covers.

- Surgical cap.

- Surgical scrub suit.

- Two pairs of surgical gloves.

Leg coverings, aprons, and other protective gear is optional but encouraged. Think of it this way. The more layers of protection you have on. The less likely it becomes that there will be an accident where body fluids come in contact with bare skin.

Put the gear on before entering the room. It should be left on the entire time you're in the room. Wrap the body in plastic and place it into a leakproof bag if you have one available. If not, wrap the body in multiple layers of plastic and tape it shut to prevent fluids from leaking out. Keep your protective gear on while you carry the bag out of the house and only remove it once you're clear of the area where the body was left. Take care not to touch the outside of the gear while removing it. Wash your hands thoroughly with soap and water and incinerate the equipment when you're done.

If possible, coordinate the transport of the remains with local or state authorities.

CHAPTER 26

Preparing an Isolation Area: Ebola Lockdown Mode

You must plan before selecting and preparing an isolation area for members of your family or a friend who may become sick with Ebola. Your isolation area should be wholly separate and well away from your primary place of residence.

During the period of your Ebola lockdown, a friend or family member may unexpectedly show up at your home and show signs and symptoms of Ebola. Others may show up with no symptoms but maybe still be infected and within the 21 day incubation period. In either case, do not let these people into your isolation area (your place of residence where healthy people reside). If you do decide that you'll want to help these people, you'll need to plan and create quarantine areas for those who are infected and for those who are potentially contaminated.

Preparing an Isolation Area for Those Potentially Infected

Your quarantine area for those who are potentially infected should be a separate area from your place of residence. This area is for those who are suspected of having Ebola but are not yet showing heavy symptoms (fever, headaches, vomiting, diarrhea). This space could be your garage or storage shed in the back yard. Contact with this person in quarantine should be minimal, and their condition should be monitored on an hourly basis. If their condition worsens and heavy symptoms of Ebola surface, they will need to be transported to the quarantine area for those who are infected.

Those who are suspected of having Ebola and are in quarantine will need to stay in quarantine for at least three weeks. If no signs or symptoms of Ebola emerge within this period, it's likely safe for them to join your whole isolation area in your place of residence. Keep in mind that this isolation area will need to have its dedicated bathroom facility as those within this area will be restricted to this area only.

This person will not be able to leave this area for at least 21 days. Entranceways should be covered with heavy plastic or a tarp and sealed with duct tape. Food and other supplies can be slipped beneath this plastic to that inside. Food should be served with disposable plates and cutlery and bagged up and burned immediately after use. If a healthy person does need to enter this area, they should cover up with approved disposable clothing (hazmat suit), gloves, shoe covers, hair cover, and an N95 face mask. Upon returning to the whole isolation area, this disposable protective clothing will be carefully disinfected and removed, bagged up in heavy garbage bags, and burned immediately.

Preparing an Isolation Area for Those Who Are Infected

For those who are showing symptoms of Ebola, they will need to be immediately quarantined from the rest of the whole group. Keep your distance from all who are infected and <u>do not</u> let them enter into your entire isolation area within your residence. Whoever becomes the dedicated caretaker of the sick will need to wear the proper Personal Protective Equipment before any direct contact takes place with those who are suffering. Be sure to disinfect any areas around the home where the infected person has been with bleach – and clean thoroughly.

The quarantine area for the sick should be set up as far away from your primary residence as possible. If this cannot be done, then a room that is completely sealed off from the rest of the house can be used. Use a heavy tarp or plastic over the doorway. Only the dedicated caretaker will be allowed to enter this area. When setting up a quarantine area within your home, the following needs to be considered:

- The room for the sick person needs to be sealed off entirely from the rest if it's located within your house. Use a place that's as far away from the first isolation area as possible. Create a decontamination area between the sick room and the rest of the home. It is where PPE and garbage will be disinfected and bagged up to be burned.

- Whoever enters into this isolation room needs to be protected entirely from head to toe with no exposed areas (more on approved PPE soon)

- Those entering into the sick area should wear an N95 mask

- The sick should use disposable cutlery and dinnerware. It needs to be bagged up and burned immediately after use.

- The sick person CANNOT leave the sick room at any time. A separate bathroom will need to be set up within their area for their use. At a minimum, a portable toilet or human waste bag will do. Running water is also a good idea to have for cleanliness.

- Cover the mattress inside the sick room with a massive plastic sheet to prevent infectious bodily fluids from soaking into the material.

- All items removed from the sick room should be handled as though they contain the virus. Any dishes or other supplies removed from the ill office should be thoroughly disinfected with a 10% bleach solution or other comparable disinfectants.

- Buy some heavy-duty freezer type zip-lock bags to dispose of tissues and other smaller items used by the sick. All beddings and clothing used by the sick should be rolled up and carefully placed into a heavy-duty garbage bag. Wash these items in boiling water using plenty of detergents to kill germs.

- Make sure your sick room is stocked up with plenty of alcohol-based hand cleanser for the sick. I have used this on hands regularly.

- All items in the sick room should be cleaned regularly with a 10% bleach solution (mixing 1 part bleach to 10 parts water). Focus mainly on things that are commonly touched by the sick person (doorknobs, faucets, toilet, tables, light switches)

- Any person entering the room should wear a PPE protective suit, foot protection, nitrile gloves, eye protection, and an N95 or N100 face mask. A face mask should be worn by the sick also when in close contact with the caretaker. All disposable PPE should be carefully removed and disposed of immediately. Wash and disinfect hand with alcohol-based hand cleanser after removing these items. All of those coming into close contact with the sick should avoid touching their mouths, eyes, and nose.

- Keep the door to the sick room closed at all times. A bell or a cell phone should be left by the bedside to allow the sick to call for assistance.

It's a good idea to stock up your quarantine areas (sick rooms) as soon as possible while supplies are still available.

Consider the following items when shopping for supplies:

- Heavy-duty plastic sheets or a tarp

- Plastic pail and dishpan

- PPE (suit, shoe covers, eye protection, nitrile gloves, N95/N100 masks)

- Single bed with beddings and pillows

- Portable toilet

- Cock radio (one that's electric and battery-powered)

- Flashlight

- Plastic garbage can line with a heavy-duty garbage bag for soiled clothes and bedding

- Hand sanitizer and bleach

- Large zip lock bags

- Medication to control fever, blood pressure, and other ailments

- cotton balls, tissues, and toilet paper

- Duct tape (for sealing doorways and ventilation outlets/inlets)

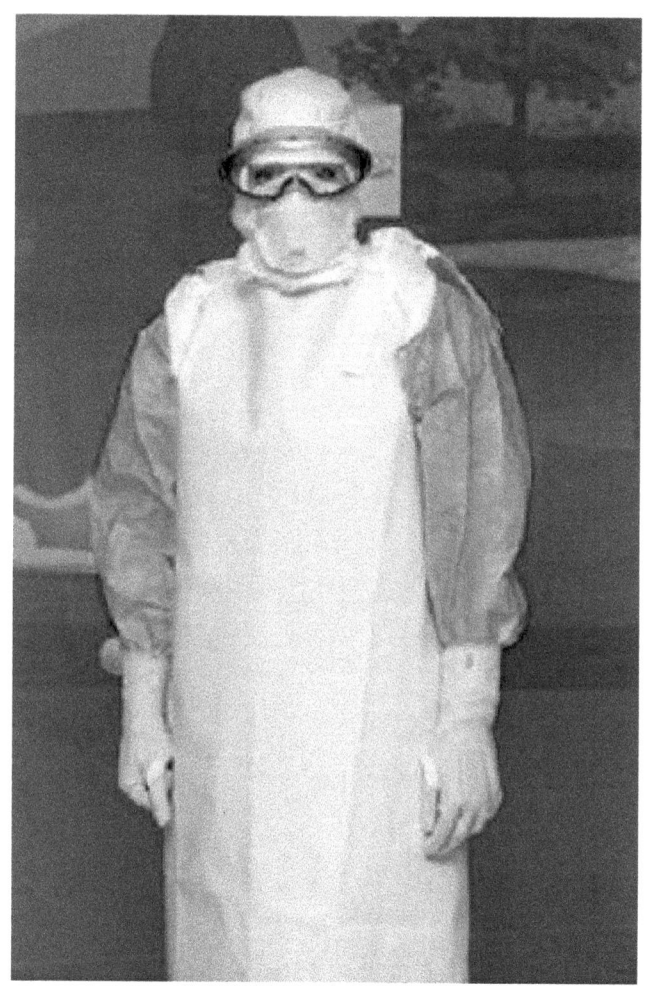

Conclusion

The 1918 influenza was the deadliest outbreak in American memory. Hundreds of thousands perished, and the extremely infectious influenza virus was transmitted by millions. Furthermore, given the magnitude of influenza in 1918, very few works have been done into the economic consequences of the pandemic. In this article, the economic impact of the influenza pandemic of 1918 was addressed and evaluated based on available data and analysis. The flu of 1918 was short-lived and had "a lasting effect not on societies, but the atoms of human society – on individuals." Although civilization as a whole quickly healed from the flu in 1918, people affected by the flu saw their lives forever altered. With our highly mobile and linked population, given advances in health care in the past 90 years, any potential pandemics of influenza will be more severe and potentially more virulent than the 1918 flu. Learning from experience might maybe serve to reduce the impact of any possible epidemic. Of necessity, it needs coordination and preparation at both levels of government and the private sector to avert a pandemic. Unfortunately, the 2005 study reveals that the United States is not preparing for an epidemic of influenza.

Although federal, state, and local governments in the U.S. have begun to focus in recent years on preparedness, progress has been slow, especially at the local government level. There's been poor coordination at various governments' levels in response to the past disaster. If people choose governments to prevent an influenza epidemic, policy preparation, and the ability to protect citizens from a pandemic should be a matter of concern. Perhaps the best way to protect citizens in the case of a potential flu pandemic is public education about flu prevention, greater reliance on charity groups and charitable organizations, and a dose of personal responsibility.

This study also found wet lungs in influenza with the primary component of swelling. The fluid would vary in color and consistency, depending on where the lung was in terms of infection and recovery. Occasionally blood would leak during an examination. The only blood vessels affected, consistent with other studies, were small ones. The distribution was concordantly strikingly irregular.

The gray period of lung injury was found to be also present in this study, and the fluid was also changed to a stickier, more mucus inconsistency. Abscesses were found in two cases, in which there was extensive tissue death. There were exciting findings of yellow patches on the pleura (lining of the lung) in advanced cases, some so widespread that it looked as if it impeded function. It was only likened to a process where the lymphatic system becomes overwhelmed.

In one case, a large blood clot was found in the lower-left lobe. This area had a surrounding area of tissue death and illness. There were several surrounding small blood vessels with the yellow clots that have been described. It was likely that this was some sort of mixture of immune tissue, mucus, and hyaline.

The presence of different stages of illness within the same lung was also found in these studies. Most frequently, the congestion and inflammatory phase were found to be universal when detected, and that when the secondary stages of lung injury occurred, they progressed at their own pace. Almost all cases were found to follow the medium-sized airways (bronchi).

One finding that differed in this study somewhat found that there was an accumulation of fluid in the areas beneath the lungs (known as the pleural cavities). The type of fluid differed depending on the patient, likely due to what stage of lung injury they were. In almost all cases, both lungs were involved.

The most common systemic (present in the whole body) finding was that of the small bleeds, especially on surfaces of the intestinal tract. The only other consistent result was swelling of the liver and, to a lesser extent, the spleen. It was concluded from this paper that the hemorrhages were a positive consequence of this illness, the lungs, stomach, and intestinal tract being particularly susceptible. The findings of muscle degeneration were also found here.

This study concluded by stating that influenza caused both a systemic illness and especially injury to the lungs and respiratory tract. It was agreed that the more body-wide effects were likely caused by some sort of toxin, during the damage to the respiratory tract likely inflammation, and secondarily, infection by a bacteria following injury. It was agreed in this paper that most cases of fatality would do so during the first 48 hours of disease. The finding of effect on skeletal muscle, particularly the abdominals, was an equally surprising and agreeable report with this study and others. The sparing of the heart and kidney was also perplexing but confirmed by this study.

Lightning Source UK Ltd.
Milton Keynes UK
UKHW020636161020
371702UK00010B/400